Life Centered Career Education

Modified Curriculum for Individuals with Moderate Disabilities

Robert J. Loyd
and
Donn E. Brolin

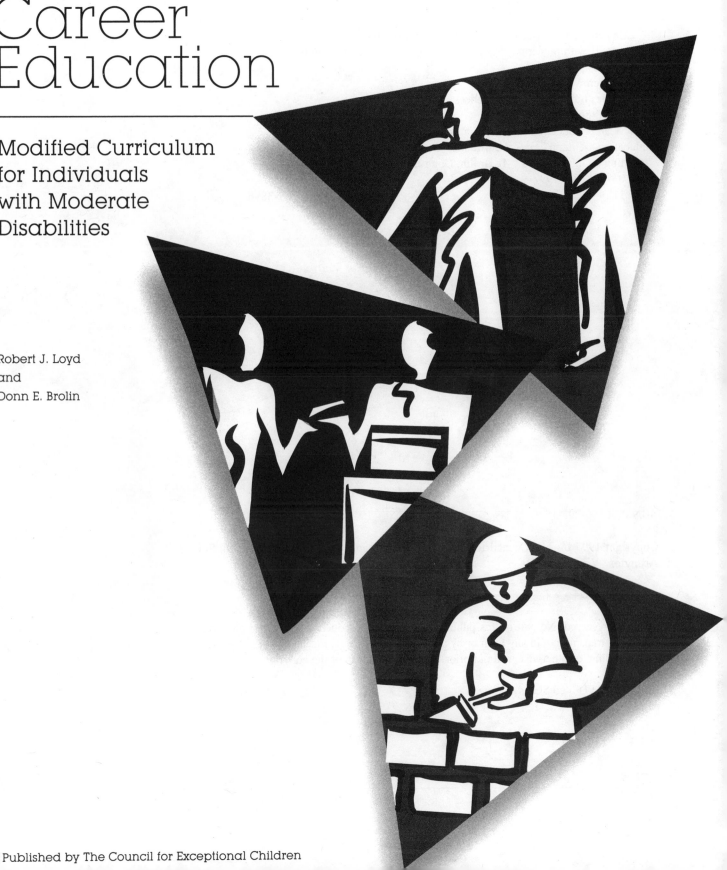

Published by The Council for Exceptional Children

Library of Congress Cataloging-in-Publication Data

Loyd, Robert J.
    Life centered career education : modified curriculum for
individuals with moderate disabilities / Robert J. Loyd and Donn E.
Brolin.
        p.   cm.
    Includes bibliographical references.
    ISBN 0-86586-293-1
    1. Career education—United States—Curricula.   2. Special
education—United States—Curricula.   3. Life skills—Study and
teaching—United States.   I. Brolin, Donn E.   II. Title.
LC1037.5.L68   1997
370.11'3—dc21
                                                                97-3896
                                            CIP

ISBN 0-86586-293-1

Copyright 1997 by The Council for Exceptional Children, 1110 North Glebe Road, Suite 300
Arlington, Virginia 22201

Stock No. P5194

Printed in the United States of America
10 9 8 7 6 5 4 3 2 1

Contents

List of Figures v

Foreword vii

1. Life Centered Career Education (LCCE) Modified Curriculum for Individuals
   with Moderate Disabilities 1

2. Instructional Implementation Strategies 8

       Daily Living Skills 12

       Personal-Social Skills 39

       Occupational Skills 63

3. Assessment and Instructional Planning Strategies 81

Appendix A: Competency Rating Scale-Modified (CRS-M) for the Life Centered Career Education (LCCE)
                   Modified Curriculum for Individuals with Moderate Disabilities 83

Appendix B: Competency Rating Scale (CRS) Master Forms for the Life Centered
                   Career Education (LCCE) Modified Curriculum for Individuals with Moderate Disabilities 91

                   Competency Rating Scale-Modified 92

Appendix C: Individualized Education Program Form-Modified 99

Appendix D: LCCE Resources Available from CEC 105

List of Figures

FIGURE 1   Correlation of Original Life Centered Career Education Competencies
and Subcompetencies with the Modified Curriculum (LCCE-M)
Competencies and Subcompetencies 5

FIGURE 2   Life Centered Career Education—Modified Curriculum (LCCE-M) 10

Competency Rating Scale-Modified (Master Forms) 92

Individualized Education Program Form-Modified (Master Forms) 99

Foreword

The Council for Exceptional Children is pleased to offer the *Life Centered Career Education: Modified Curriculum for Individuals with Moderate Disabilities.* This work supports CEC's policy on career education, which states that career education is the totality of experiences through which one learns to live a meaningful, satisfying work life. Within the career education structure, work is conceptualized as conscious effort aimed at producing benefits for oneself and/or others. Career education provides the opportunity for individuals to learn, in the least restrictive environment possible, the academic, daily living, personal-social, and occupational knowledge and the specific vocational skills necessary for attaining their highest levels of economic, personal, and social fulfillment.

CEC supports the belief that career education should permeate the entire school program and even extend beyond it. It should be infused throughout the curriculum by knowledgeable teachers who are able to modify the curriculum to integrate career development goals with existing subject matter goals and content. It is the position of the Council that individualized appropriate education for individuals with exceptionalities must include the opportunity for every student to attain his or her highest level of career potential through career education experiences. Children with exceptionalities require career education experiences that will develop to the fullest extent possible their wide range of abilities, needs, and interests.

In order to assist students with exceptionalities to become productive workers and independent adults, special education needs to work in collaboration with parents, other educators, community services, and business. The LCCE approach serves as a model for making this happen.

This piece of the LCCE line of products has been in development and field testing for several years. During the spring of 1995 more than 40 sites field-tested portions of the curriculum with their students. The feedback from these practitioners was incorporated into the final version of this product. Throughout the developmental phases of the curriculum, Dr. Loyd and Dr. Brolin worked in close collaboration, ensuring that the modified curriculum remained consistent with the original LCCE curriculum product. Because of the long history of collaboration, Dr. Loyd was able to bring this modified curriculum to completion in spite of the untimely death of Donn Brolin in 1996.

The authors would also like to acknowledge the assistance of Robert McMullan, Project Research Assistant, for his contributions to this publication.

CEC is proud to provide this modified LCCE curriculum for use in schools and adult training environments.

1. Life Centered Career Education (LCCE) Modified Curriculum for Individuals with Moderate Disabilities

The *Life Centered Career Education (LCCE) Modified Curriculum for Individuals with Moderate Disabilities* (herein referred to as the LCCE Modified Curriculum) Program (3-21+) is a modified version of the popular and widely implemented functional *Life Centered Career Education* (LCCE) curriculum program for individuals with mild disabilities (herein referred to as the "original LCCE Curriculum"). This similarly designed modified curriculum and assessment version utilizes the same competency-based framework and formatting as the original LCCE Curriculum. The LCCE Modified Curriculum program adds to the original LCCE Curriculum program continuum a competency-based functional component for individuals at a lower level of functioning (see Figure 1).

The major difference between the original and the modified LCCE Curriculum programs is that the latter focuses on the critical skills and outcomes that individuals with moderate disabilities need to assist them in making the successful transition from school to work and community living. This LCCE Modified Curriculum retains the scope and sequencing procedures found in the original LCCE Curriculum that requires teachers/trainers to match the appropriate level of subcompetency instruction/training to the individual's stage of career development (awareness, exploration, preparation, and career assimilation). This career stage approach pro-

vides a sequential framework for teaching/training the competencies and subcompetencies at all grade levels and community need levels, as well as permitting older individuals an opportunity to experience a sequential career development approach. The LCCE Modified Curriculum's instructional/training activities have been designed to promote the acquisition and performance of critical skills and outcomes needed to succeed in school, at home, in the community, and in employment settings. Another significant difference is that attention to both needed support and participation levels is embedded into the curriculum activities. Each subcompetency includes activities that the teacher/trainer will address with each individual to encourage him or her to seek assistance and support when needed.

The original LCCE Curriculum, developed by Donn E. Brolin, was first published by The Council for Exceptional Children (CEC) in 1978. This functional curriculum program is a K–12+ scope and sequenced education system designed to provide special education and other "at-risk" students with the important skills needed to function successfully as productive workers in school, home, and community environments. The original LCCE Curriculum instructional and assessment materials are grounded in more than 21 years of research. All of the materials have been widely field tested in schools and with students from all across the country. Many schools in the United States and internationally have adopted the original LCCE Curriculum as their functional/transitional special education curriculum.

NEED FOR LCCE MODIFIED CURRICULUM

Recent follow-up studies and expert opinion clearly reveal the difficulty adults with moderate disabilities have in achieving successful and appropriate levels of adult community living and working (Bates, 1986; Bellamy, 1986; Frank & Sitlington, 1993; Morgan, Moore, McSweyn, & Salzberg, 1992; Snell, 1988; Wehman & Hill, 1985). After leaving formal education programs, individuals with moderate disabilities often (a) are unemployed or severely underemployed, (b) do not participate in community living activities, and (c) do not receive appropriate postsecondary training and support services (Frank & Sitlington, 1993). It has been reported that approximately 80 to 95% of adults with moderate disabilities are unemployed or severely underemployed (Crites, Small, & Sachs, 1985). These poor employment adult outcomes result in individuals who must depend on additional supplemental funding programs for their subsistence.

In the Iowa special education follow-up study, Sitlington, Frank, and Carson (1993) interviewed approximately 600 school leavers with mild and moderate disabilities, who left school during the 1985 and 1986 school years, to determine their transitional adult outcomes. It was found that only 10% of the individuals with moderate disabilities were living independently without support. Most were still living with parents or relatives. The researchers also determined that the majority of this population's income came from the supplemental security income (SSI) program. This follow-up study reported that over 75% of these school leavers had not participated in any postsecondary education since leaving school. At the time of the interview, only one was working in competitive employment. The others were employed in sheltered employment and reported making less than $1.00 an hour. The most significant recommendation the study provided was to have schools begin functional curriculum implementation at the elementary school level. The researchers also recommended that a significant community-based and home component be included in these students' functional/transitional programs. Empowering students to become more involved in their own self-advocacy and career path options development during the elementary school years was another significant recommendation provided by the study.

Rusch (1986) also reported the poor transitional outcomes these same individuals were experiencing after leaving formalized education. He described this situation as a critical concern in the education of individuals with moder-

ate disabilities and recommended that schools start implementing the "best practices" identified in model transition demonstration programs. His recommendation, along with other research studies, concurred with the Iowa special education follow-up study that there is a critical need for schools to begin implementing competency-based and community-based functional curriculum programs (Enchelmaier, Kohler, & Rusch, 1994; Johnson & Rusch, 1993; Kohler, 1993; Morgan et al., 1992).

The career education research literature has for years expressed the need for the development of an appropriate functional curriculum program. This expressed need led to the development and wide implementation of the original LCCE Curriculum program. This 21+-year program for students with mild disabilities has now been modified and expanded. The LCCE Modified Curriculum has been developed to meet the field's need for a functional, transitional, and community-based curriculum geared toward individuals with moderate disabilities.

ORIGINAL LCCE CURRICULUM MODIFICATION PROCESS

The original LCCE Curriculum program, which spans a 21-year developmental period, has gone through several revisions and modifications. The original LCCE Curriculum competencies and subcompetencies have been revised twice. The LCCE Modified Curriculum for individuals with moderate disabilities is an extension and revision of the original LCCE Curriculum. All revisions to the original LCCE Curriculum were a result of the findings from field-validation research studies. The primary purpose of these studies was to determine whether the field felt that the curriculum's competencies, subcompetencies, and objectives were still appropriate. A field-validation research study was also conducted to determine whether the curriculum's competencies, subcompetencies, and objectives were appropriate for individuals with moderate disabilities. Each field-validation research study resulted in minor changes to the original LCCE Curriculum and substantial changes for the LCCE Modified Curriculum for individuals with moderate disabilities. The first LCCE Curriculum (1978) had 22 major competencies, 102 subcompetencies, and 3 to 8 objectives for each subcompetency. The original LCCE Curriculum's revision in 1982 resulted in minor changes in a couple of the competencies and a reduction of the subcompetencies from 102 to the current 97. There are approximately 425 total objectives for the original LCCE Curriculum. Each research project also resulted in revisions to the curriculum guides. See the original LCCE Curriculum guide for a complete description and listing of the available LCCE Curriculum instructional and assessment materials.

LCCE MODIFIED CURRICULUM RESEARCH PROJECT

This LCCE Modified Curriculum resulted from a need expressed by professionals and practitioners who educate/train individuals with moderate disabilities. Throughout the 21-year span of LCCE Curriculum development and use, LCCE staff received numerous requests from across the country to study the feasibility of having a separate LCCE Curriculum designed specifically for individuals with moderate disabilities. Prior to the development of the LCCE Modified Curriculum, project staff encouraged teachers who were requesting a modified version to develop their own modified LCCE Curriculum for this population. Although many teachers did make some modifications to the original LCCE Curriculum for individuals with moderate disabilities, most felt that a stand-alone, field-validated curriculum program would be more effective and beneficial for this population. This prompted the LCCE staff to design and implement a research project to study the feasibility and appropriateness of modifying the original LCCE Curriculum.

This research project's purpose was designed to (a) determine whether a sample of practitioners, parents, and agencies felt that the original LCCE Curriculum needed to be modified for this population and, if so, (b) determine just what modifications would be necessary to make the curriculum more appropriate for this population. The research project utilized the same methodology and analysis as the earlier federally funded field-validated curriculum evaluation research projects.

METHOD

The research project encompassed five major activities. Deciding on the appropriate research design was the first project activity. A modified Delphi survey was selected to determine whether the original LCCE Curriculum needed to be modified and, if so, to indicate the LCCE Modified Curriculum's specific competencies, subcompetencies, and objectives. Project staff decided to use the same survey instrument as was used in the previously conducted LCCE Curriculum evaluation research projects. They felt that it would be appropriate to use the same instrument since both projects addressed the same research questions and only differed in the curriculum's intended population. This survey instrument had been reviewed by national experts, field piloted, and validated during the earlier research projects. Respondents, who assisted or were familiar with individuals who have moderate disabilities, were given an opportunity on the survey to analyze the appropriateness of the original LCCE Curriculum for individuals with moderate disabilities and then to suggest any necessary modifications. Only the

introduction section of the original survey had to be revised. The survey's revised introduction section explained the purpose of the study and asked survey respondents to indicate (a) whether the original LCCE Curriculum competencies were appropriate for this other population and, if not, to suggest a more appropriate competency; (b) whether the original LCCE Curriculum subcompetencies were appropriate and, if not, to suggest a more appropriate subcompetency; and (c) if the subcompetencies were revised to suggest a list of objectives needed to master or perform the subcompetency.

Deciding upon a study sample was the second research activity. Project staff selected the following research sample: 250 teachers who teach students with moderate disabilities, 250 family representatives who had children with moderate disabilities, and 250 agency personnel who provide service to children and adults with moderate disabilities. Surveys were either mailed or personally delivered to the respondents. Project staff made oral presentations to some groups, who then completed the surveys either after the presentation or at later times. Mailings to large groups also included a videotape explaining the survey and directions for completion. Follow-up telephone calls were made to the mailed survey respondents to ascertain their understanding of the survey and completion procedures. As a result of this more personalized administration procedure, project staff received a high survey return rate. Approximately 500 usable surveys were collected for analysis (67%).

The returned first-round surveys were then analyzed to determine whether respondents felt there was a need to modify the original LCCE Curriculum to make it more appropriate for individuals with moderate disabilities. Almost all of the survey respondents (94%) felt that modifications to the original LCCE Curriculum were necessary and that there was a need to develop a separate LCCE Curriculum modified for use with individuals who have moderate disabilities. Based on the findings and recommendations from this first-round survey, major modifications were made to the original LCCE Curriculum's competencies, subcompetencies, and objectives. A second-round survey based on the modifications was prepared and administered to 150 selected first-round respondents. Project staff personally administered this second-round survey to a selected group of 75 teachers, 50 parents, and 25 agency personnel. The analysis of the second-round surveys resulted in minor revisions to the LCCE Modified Curriculum. This revised LCCE Modified Curriculum was then presented to a panel of experts in the field for their review. The experts suggested some additional minor revisions, resulting in the current LCCE Modified Curriculum for Individuals with Moderate Disabilities.

This field-developed LCCE Modified Curriculum consists of a modified set of the original LCCE Curriculum's competencies, subcompetencies, and objectives. Many of the competency and subcompetency revisions are minor, but consensus from the field indicates that this curriculum reflects a more community-based and performance-related orientation, which is more appropriate for this population.

Developing this curriculum guide was the final research project activity. The guide contains this overview (Chapter 1), the suggested instructional/training activities and implementation strategies (Chapter 2), assessment and instructional planning strategies (Chapter 3), and the Competency Rating Scale (CRS) (Appendix A). The instructional/training activities for each of the subcompetency objectives were developed for implementation in both school and community-based environments.

RESULTS

The LCCE Modified Curriculum validation research study resulted in substantial modifications being made to the original LCCE Curriculum's competencies, subcompetencies, and objectives. These revisions included changing from 22 to 20 major competencies along with changes in the competency titles. The subcompetency revisions also involved title changes, and the total number of subcompetencies changed from 97 to 75. Objectives were also modified to correspond to the revisions made in the subcompetencies. Figure 1 shows the Modified Curriculum along with the corresponding competencies from the original LCCE Curriculum.

SUMMARY

The LCCE Modified Curriculum is a scope and sequenced functional curriculum designed for use with individuals who have moderate disabilities. Although this program was developed specifically for this population, consumers may find it appropriate to use with other disabled and/or nondisabled populations. This program adds an additional functional curriculum component to the original LCCE Curriculum program continuum. Individuals with moderate disabilities who complete this curriculum program are encouraged to continue, if appropriate, their functional school- and community-based training in any part or with all of the original LCCE Curriculum program.

REFERENCES

Bates, P. (1986). Competitive employment in southern Illinois. In F. Rusch (Ed.), *Competitive employment: Issues and strategies* (pp. 51–63). Baltimore: Paul H. Brookes.

Bellamy, T. (1986). Severe disability in adulthood. *Newsletter of the Association for Persons with Severe Handicaps, 11,* 6.

Brolin, D. E. (1997). *Life Centered Career Education: A competency based approach,* 5th ed. Reston, VA: The Council for Exceptional Children.

Crites, L., Small, M., & Sachs, M. (1985). Demographic and functional characteristics of respondents to the mentally retarded community needs survey: Persons living at home with the family. Unpublished manuscript, University of Maryland School of Medicine, Baltimore.

Enchelmaier, J., Kohler, P., & Rusch, F. (1994). Employment outcomes and activities for youths in transition. *Career Education for Exceptional Individuals. 17*(1), 1–16.

Frank, A. R., & Sitlington, P. L. (1993). Graduates with mental disabilities: The story three years later. *Education and Training in Mental Retardation, 28*(1), 30–37.

Johnson, J. R., & Rusch, F. R. (1993). Secondary special education and transition services: Identification and recommendations for future research and demonstration. *Career Education for Exceptional Individuals, 16*(1), 1–18.

Kohler, P. D. (1993). Best practices in transition: Substantiated or implied? *Career Development for Exceptional Individuals, 16*(2), 107–122.

Morgan, R. L., Moore, S. C., McSweyn, C. A., & Salzberg, C. L. (1992). Transition from school to work: Views of secondary special educators. *Education and Training in Mental Retardation, 27*(4), 315–323.

Rusch, F. (1986). *Competitive employment: Issues and strategies.* Baltimore: Paul H. Brookes.

Sitlington, R., Frank, A., & Carson, R. (1993). Adult adjustment among high school graduates with mild disabilities. *Exceptional Children, 59,* 221–233.

Snell, M. (1988). Curriculum and methodology for individuals with severe disabilities. *Education and Training in Mental Retardation, 23*(4), 302–314.

Wehman, P., & Hill, J. (1985). *Competitive employment for persons with mental retardation.* Richmond: Virginia Commonwealth University.

Wehman, P., Kregel, J., & Barcus, J. (1985). School-to-work: A vocational transition model for handicapped youth. In P. Wehman and J. W. Hewitt (Eds.). *Competitive employment for persons with mental retardation: From research to practice.* Richmond: Virginia. Commonwealth University.

FIGURE 1

Correlation of Original Life Centered Career Education Competencies and Subcompetencies with the Modified Curriculum (LCCE-M) Competencies and Subcompetencies

Modified LCCE   *Original LCCE*

Daily Living Skills

1. Managing Money
    1. Count money
    2. Make purchases
    3. Use vending machines
    4. Budget money
    5. Perform banking skills

2. Selecting and Maintaining Living Environments
    6. Select appropriate community living environments
    7. Maintain living environment
    8. Use basic appliances and tools
    9. Set up personal living space

3. Caring for Personal Health
    10. Perform appropriate grooming and hygiene
    11. Dress appropriately
    12. Maintain physical fitness

    13. Recognize and seek help for illness

    14. Practice basic first aid
    15. Practice personal safety

4. Developing and Maintaining Appropriate Intimate Relationships
    16. Demonstrate knowledge of basic human sexuality
    17. Demonstrate knowledge of appropriate dating behavior

5. Eating at Home and in the Community
    18. Plan balanced meals
    19. Purchase food
    20. Prepare meals
    21. Demonstrate appropriate eating habits
    22. Demonstrate meal clean-up and food storage
    23. Demonstrate appropriate restaurant dining

6. Cleaning and Purchasing Clothing
    24. Wash/dry clothes
    25. Buy clothes

7. Participate in Leisure/Recreational Activities
    26. Identify available community leisure/recreational activities

    27. Select and plan leisure/recreational activities
    28. Participate in individual and group leisure/recreational activities
    29. Select and participate in group travel

8. Getting Around in the Community
    30. Follow traffic rules and safety procedures
    31. Develop and follow community access routes
    32. Access available transportation

1. Managing Personal Finances
    1. Count money and make correct change
    2. Make responsible expenditures

    3. Keep basic financial records
    6. Use banking services

2. Selecting and Managing a Household
    9. Select adequate housing
    7. Maintain home exterior/interior
    8. Use basic appliances and tools
    10. Set up a household

3. Caring for Personal Needs
    13. Exhibit proper grooming and hygiene
    14. Dress appropriately
    12. Demonstrate knowledge of physical fitness, nutrition, and weight
    15. Demonstrate knowledge of common illness prevention and treatment

    16. Practice personal safety

4. Raising Children and Meeting Marriage Responsibilities
    19. Demonstrate marriage responsibilities
    57. Establish and maintain close relationships

5. Buying, Preparing, and Consuming Food
    25. Plan/eat balanced meals
    20. Purchase food
    23. Prepare meals
    24. Demonstrate appropriate eating habits
    21. Clean food preparation areas; 22. Store food

6. Buying and Caring for Clothing
    26. Wash/clean clothing
    27. Purchase clothing

8. Utilizing Recreational Facilities and Engaging in Leisure
    33. Demonstrate knowledge of available community resources
    34. Choose and plan activities
    36. Engage in group and individual activities

    37. Plan vacation time

9. Getting Around the Community
    38. Demonstrate knowledge of traffic and safety
    40. Find way around the community
    39. Demonstrate knowledge and use of various means of transportation

FIGURE 1 *Continued*

Modified LCCE	*Original LCCE*

Personal-Social Skills

9. Acquiring Self-Identity

    33. Demonstrate knowledge of personal interests and abilities
    34. Demonstrate appropriate responses to emotions
    35. Display self-confidence and self-worth

    36. Demonstrate giving and accepting praise and criticism

10. Exhibiting Socially Responsible Behavior
    37. Demonstrate appropriate behavior
    38. Identify current and future personal roles
    39. Demonstrate respect for others' rights and property
    40. Demonstrate respect for authority
    41. Demonstrate ability to follow directions/instructions
    42. Demonstrate appropriate citizen rights and responsibilities

    43. Identify how personal behavior affects others

11. Developing and Maintaining Appropriate Social Relationships
    44. Develop friendships
    45. Maintain friendships

12. Exhibiting Independent Behavior
    46. Set and reach personal goals
    47. Demonstrate self-organization
    48. Demonstrate self-determination

13. Making Informed Decisions
    49. Identify problems/conflicts
    50. Use appropriate resources to assist in problem solving
    51. Develop and select best solution to problems/conflicts
    52. Demonstrate decision making

14. Communicating with Others
    53. Demonstrate listening and responding skills
    54. Demonstrate effective communication
    55. Communicate in emergency situations

---

10. Achieving Self-Awareness; 11. Acquiring Self-Confidence
    43. Identify interests and abilities
    44. Identify emotions
    47. Express feelings of self-worth; 50. Develop confidence in oneself
    48. Accept and give praise; 49. Accept and give criticism

12. Achieving Socially Responsible Behavior
    53. Demonstrate appropriate behavior in public places
    55. Recognize personal roles
    51. Develop respect for the rights and property of others
    52. Recognize authority and follow instructions

    32. Demonstrate knowledge of citizens' rights and responsibilities
    61. Demonstrate awareness of how one's behavior affects others

13. Maintaining Good Interpersonal Skills
    58. Make and maintain friendships

14. Achieving Independence
    66. Develop goal-seeking behavior
    60. Demonstrate self-organization

15. Making Adequate Decisions
    65. Recognize nature of problems
    62. Locate and utilize sources of assistance
    64. Develop and evaluate alternatives
    63. Anticipate consequences

16. Communicating with Others
    56. Demonstrate listening and responding skills
    68. Communicate with understanding
    67. Recognize and respond to emergency situations

Occupational Guidance and Preparation

15. Exploring and Locating Occupational Training and Job Placement Opportunities
    56. Identify rewards of working

    57. Locate available occupational training and job placement possibilities

16. Making Occupational and Job Placement Choices
    58. Demonstrate knowledge of occupational interests
    59. Demonstrate knowledge of occupational strengths and weaknesses
    60. Identify possible and available jobs matching interests and strengths
    61. Plan and make realistic occupational training and job placement decisions
    62. Develop training plan for occupational choice

17. Applying for and Maintaining Occupational Training and Job Placements
    63. Apply for occupational training and job placements
    64. Interview for occupational training and job placements
    65. Make adjustments to changes in employment status

18. Developing and Maintaining Appropriate Work Skills and Behavior
    66. Perform work directions and requirements
    67. Maintain good attendance and punctuality
    68. Respond appropriately to supervision
    69. Demonstrate job safety
    70. Work cooperatively with others
    71. Meet quality and quantity work standards

19. Matching Physical-Manual Skills to Occupational Training and Employment
    72. Demonstrate fine motor dexterity in occupational and job placements
    73. Demonstrate gross motor dexterity in occupational training and job placements
    74. Demonstrate sensory discrimination in occupational training and job placements
    75. Demonstrate stamina and endurance

20. Training and Occupational Choices

17. Knowing and Exploring Occupational Possibilities

    70. Identify remunerative aspects of work; 72.Identify personal values met through work; 73. Identify societal values met through work
    71. Locate sources of occupational and training information; 74. Classify jobs into occupational categories; 75. Investigate local occupational and training opportunities

18. Selecting and Planning Occupational Choices
    79. Identify major occupational interests
    78. Identify occupational aptitudes

    77. Identify requirements of appropriate and available jobs
    76. Make realistic occupational choices

20. Seeking, Securing, and Maintaining Employment

    89. Apply for a job
    90. Interview for a job
    93. Know how to adjust to change in employment

19. Exhibiting Appropriate Work Habits and Behavior

    81. Follow directions and observe regulations
    82. Recognize importance of attendance and punctuality
    83. Recognize importance of supervision
    84. Demonstrate knowledge of occupational safety
    85. Work with others
    86. Meet demands of quality work; 87. Work at a satisfactory rate

21. Exhibiting Sufficient Physical/Manual Skills

    96. Demonstrate manual dexterity

    97. Demonstrate sensory discrimination

    94. Demonstrate stamina and endurance

22. Obtaining a Specific Occupational Skill

There are no specific subcompetencies listed here since they depend upon the specific occupational training selected.

2. Instructional Implementation Strategies

This chapter presents the guidelines for implementing the instructional strategies and activities for the LCCE Modified Curriculum. The curriculum outlines the instructional/training strategies and activities for teaching each one of the LCCE Modified Curriculum's 20 major competencies, 75 subcompetencies, and their objectives. This curriculum guide employs the same format and guidelines as the original LCCE Curriculum guide.

STRUCTURE OF CURRICULUM GUIDE

Each one of the 75 subcompetencies in the curriculum guide provides the following three specific components: (1) a list of the objectives that are necessary for subcompetency mastery, (2) school training activities, and (3) home/community-based training activities. These three components are designed to assist teachers, family members, and community service personnel to provide individuals with moderate disabilities with relevant performance experiences for achieving mastery of the 20 competencies and 75 subcompetencies. No specific grade or age level is suggested for subcompetency training. Instruction is to be designed and implemented based on individual needs. Assessment of specific individual needs can be determined by administering the Competency Rating Scale-Modified (CRS-M) (see Appendix A). The CRS-M and LCCE Modified Curriculum assessment strategies and instructional planning are discussed in Chapter 3.

Objectives

Each subcompetency includes two to six performance objectives that must be mastered to demonstrate subcompetency acquisition. Objectives can be expanded and/or developed in smaller units to meet specific individual needs of each student with moderate disabilities. Additional objectives can also be developed if necessary.

Training Activities

Training activities are the vehicle by which teachers convey the information to develop subcompetency acquisition. The suggested training activities are not arranged in any hierarchy, although some consideration must be given to identifying the difficulty of any activity. More appropriate training activities may be developed and included. The suggested training activities make use of a wide array of resources and supports. Emphasis on generalization is recommended to ensure transfer of performance in natural settings. These activities include roleplays, discussions, guest speakers, developing collages, and so forth.

A unique feature in this curriculum is that, for each of the subcompetencies, students are taught to seek assistance and support when needed. This student empowerment strategy has been embedded into the curriculum to prepare the students to request the supports they need for integration into normalized environments.

Home-/Community-Based Training Activities

It is strongly suggested that these activities be given priority as students/individuals move into higher grades or age levels. These activities are critical in assisting students/individuals with moderate disabilities to achieve a successful transition from school to work and community living. Also, it is strongly suggested that parents and other family members be involved in home-/community-based training. These activities include roleplays, discussions, job shadows, hands-on experience, and the like.

Integration

The successful implementation of this curriculum will require attention to instruction in natural environments. It is strongly suggested that instruction *always* take place in the least restrictive integrated environments. This usually can, and in most instances should, occur in normalized community environments. Finally, instructors/trainers should pay careful attention to addressing the current and future ecological environments, instructional needs, generalization/transfer of skills, and maintenance of skills of individuals with moderate disabilities. Implementation of these strategies is critical to ensure that students succeed in making the necessary transition.

Guidelines for Effective Use of Curriculum Guide

Effective instruction using the curriculum guide is contingent on certain conditions or factors. As with any training activity, teachers and support personnel must make individualized decisions about student needs and the instruction necessary to meet those needs. Several factors to consider when using the curriculum guide include (a) using age-appropriate materials; (b) teaching for generalization; (c) utilizing individual strengths and weaknesses; (d) utilizing home and community supports; (e) providing instruction in integrative and natural community environments; (f) actively involving and empowering the individual in the development and implementation of his or her functional individualized education program (IEP) and instructional program; (g) implementing self-advocacy strategies, training, and activities; and (h) actively involving family members and community supports.

The training activities and home/community-based training activities presented in the following section are intended to serve as a guide for teaching the 20 competencies and 75 subcompetencies. We believe that these activities will result in more successful transitional adult outcomes for individuals with moderate disabilities.

FIGURE 2
Life Centered Career Education—Modified Curriculum (LCCE-M)

Curriculum Area	Competency	Subcompetency: The student will be able to:	
DAILY LIVING SKILLS	1. Managing Money	1. Count Money	2. Make purchases
	2. Selecting and Maintaining Living Environments	6. Select appropriate community living environment	7. Maintain living environment
	3. Caring for Personal Health	10. Perform appropriate grooming and hygiene	11. Dress appropriately
	4. Developing and Maintaining Appropriate Intimate Relationships	16. Demonstrate knowledge of basic human sexuality	17. Demonstrate knowledge of appropriate dating behavior
	5. Eating at Home and in the Community	18. Plan balanced meals	19. Purchase food
	6. Cleaning and Purchasing Clothing	24. Wash/dry clothes	25. Buy clothes
	7. Participate in Leisure/ Recreational Activities	26. Identify available community leisure/recreational activities	27. Select and plan leisure/recreational activities
	8. Getting Around in the Community	30. Follow traffic rules and safety procedures	31. Develop and follow community access routes
PERSONAL-SOCIAL SKILLS	9. Acquiring Self-Identity	33. Demonstrate knowledge of personal interests and abilities	34. Demonstrate appropriate responses to emotions
	10. Exhibiting Socially Responsible Behavior	37. Demonstrate appropriate behavior	38. Identify current and future personal roles
	11. Developing and Maintaining Appropriate Social Relationships	44. Develop friendships	45. Maintain friendships
	12. Exhibiting Independent Behavior	46. Set and reach personal goals	47. Demonstrate self-organization
	13. Making Informed Decisions	49. Identify problems/conflicts	50. Use appropriate resources to assist in problem-solving
	14. Communiciating with Others	53. Demonstrate listening and responding skills	54. Demonstrate effective communication
OCCUPATIONAL GUIDANCE AND PREPARATION	15. Exploring and Locating Occupational Training and Job Placement Opportunities	56. Identify rewards of working	57. Locate occupational training and job placement possibilities
	16. Making Occupational and Job Placement Choices	58. Demonstrate knowledge of occupational interests	59. Demonstrate knowledge of occupational strengths and weaknesses
	17. Applying for and Maintaining Occupatioinal Training and Job Placements	63. Apply for occupational training and job placements	64. Interview for occupational training and job placements
	18. Developing and Maintaining Appropriate Work Skills and Behavior	66. Perform work directions and requirements	67. Maintain good attendance and punctuality
	19. Matching Physical-Manual Skills to Occupational Training and Employment	72. Demonstrate fine motor dexterity in occupational training & job placements	73. Demonstrate gross motor dexterity in occupational training & job placements
	20. Training and Occupational Choices		

3. Use vending machine	4. Budget money	5. Perform banking skills		
8. Use basic appliances and tools	9. Set up personal living space			
12. Maintain physical fitness	13. Recognize and seek help for illness	14. Practice basic first aid	15. Practice personal safety	
20. Prepare meals	21. Demonstrate appropriate eating habits	22. Demonstrate meal clean-up and food storage	23. Demonstrate appropriate restaurant dining	
28. Participate in individual and group leisure/ recreational activities	29. Select and participate in group travel			
32. Access available transportation				
35. Display self-confidence and self-worth	36. Demonstrate giving and accepting praise and criticism			
39. Demonstrate respect for others' rights and property	40. Demonstrate respect for authority	41. Demonstrate ability to follow directions/ instructions	42. Demonstrate appropriate citizen rights and responsibilities	43. Identify how personal behavior affects others
48. Demonstrate self-determination				
51. Develop and select best solution to problems/conflicts	52. Demonstrate decision-making			
55. Communicate in emergency situations				
60. Identify possible and available matching interests and strengths	61. Plan and make realistic occupational training and job placement decisions	62. Develop training plan for occupational choice		
65. Make adjustments to changes in employment status				
68. Respond appropriately to supervision	69. Demonstrate job safety	70. Work cooperatively with others	71. Meet quality and quantity work standards	
74. Demonstrate sensory discrimination in occupational training & job placements	75. Demonstrate stamina and endurance			
There are no specific subcompetencies listed here since they depend upon the specific occupational training selected.				

DAILY LIVING SKILLS

Domain: Daily Living Skills
Competency 1: Managing Money
Subcompetency 1: Count Money

Objectives	Training Activities	Home-/Community-Based Training Activities
1. Identify coins	• Student discusses names of all coin types • Student finds penny, nickel, dime, quarter, and half dollar from an assortment of coins • Student names all coin types	• Student names the coins from adult's/peer's pocket change • Student names the coins used during adult's/peer's transactions
2. Count sums of up to five coins from stacks of pennies, nickels, dimes, quarters, and half dollars	• Student collects and counts up to five like coins • Student counts sums of up to five coins • Student collects and counts up to five different coins • Student seeks assistance from teacher	• Student counts the value of two to five coins from adult's/peer's change • Student seeks assistance from adult/peer
3. Identify bills up to $20	• Student identifies one-, five-, ten-, and twenty-dollar bills by recognizing denomination • Student finds one-, five-, ten-, and twenty-dollar bills from a stack of different bills • Student seeks assistance from teacher	• Student names currency from adult's/peer's wallet • Student names the currency used during adult's/peer's transactions in the community • Student seeks assistance from adult/peer
4. Count currency with sums less than $20	• Student counts like bills with sums up to $20 • Student practices counting bills up to sums of $20 • Student counts different bills with sums up to $20 • Student seeks assistance from teacher	• Student counts bills up to sums of $20 with adult/peer at home and in the community • Student seeks assistance from adult/peer

Domain: Daily Living Skills
Competency 1: Managing Money
Subcompetency 2: Make Purchases

Objectives	Training Activities	Home-/Community-Based Training Activities
1. Select appropriate items	• Student finds items named by teacher in school store, food mart, drugstores, grocery stores, and other community retail stores/businesses • Student selects appropriate items from teacher list	• Student makes up a list for grocery stores, drugstores, and other community retail stores/businesses with adult/peer • Student selects appropriate items when requested by adult/peer
2. Recognize and request assistance	• Student finds pictures of store clerk in magazines or "world of work" textbooks • Student finds store clerk in retail store/business • Student discusses and roleplays problem situations that require help, finds appropriate source of help, decides when to ask, and then requests assistance for problem	• Student discusses ways to identify store clerks in retail store/business with adult/peer • Student finds store clerk and requests help in finding appropriate items with adult/peer

	Training Activities	Home-/Community-Based Training Activities
	• Student recognizes and requests assistance from student named as the clerk in the school store	
3. Locate cashier	• Student finds picture of cashier in magazines or "world of work" textbooks and books • Student finds cash register with light/signal or cashier in several retail stores/businesses • Student seeks assistance from teacher	• Student locates cashier in retail store/business with adult/peer • Student finds appropriate cash register or cashier in retail store/business with adult/peer • Student seeks assistance from adult/peer
4. Calculate and give appropriate purchase amount	• Student uses "next dollar" method in school store, food marts, drugstores, grocery stores, and other community retail stores/businesses • Student writes check for amount of purchase on cash register/tape/receipt (SEE Competency 1, Subcompetency 5). • Student seeks assistance from teacher	• Student uses "next dollar" method in food marts, drugstores, grocery stores, and other community retail stores/businesses with adult/peer • Student practices using correct amount of purchase money at retail stores/businesses • Student writes check for amount of purchase on cash register/tape/receipt • Student seeks assistance from adult/peer
5. Receive purchase and change	• Student waits for and accepts purchase and change at school store, food marts, drugstores, grocery stores, and other community retail stores/businesses • Student role plays making purchase and waits for purchase and receives change • Student seeks assistance from teacher	• Student waits for and accepts purchase and change at food marts, drugstores, grocery stores, and other community retail stores/businesses, and checks for correct change returned with adult/peer • Student seeks assistance from adult/peer

Domain: Daily Living Skills
Competency 1: Managing Money
Subcompetency 3: Use Vending Machines

Objectives	Training Activities	Home-/Community-Based Training Activities
1. Select appropriate coins	• Student uses "four quarters" method in school and in the community (method: put quarter(s) in machine and push button after each quarter until item is received), always checking coin return • Student selects appropriate coins for use in making vending machine selection	• Student uses "four quarters" method in vending machine and pushes button after each quarter to check to see if item is received, always checking coin return • Student waits for items to be received with adult/peer
2. Operate vending machines	• Student selects and cuts out vending item from magazine pictures • Student verbally selects letters and/or numbers of wanted pictured items on vending machine • Student selects wanted item and inserts money and pushes button to operate school vending machine	• Student pushes correct numbers or letters of item wanted in machine, after inserting money into machine with adult/peer • Student operates vending machine in the community or at job placement setting
3. Receive vending machine purchase and change	• Student finds and points to the coin return/change box on school vending machine • Student finds and points to the item	• Student removes the purchased item and checks coin return/change box for change returned with adult/peer in the community

DAILY LIVING SKILLS

	dispensing area on school vending machine	• Student removes purchased item and checks coin return/change box for returned change in the community
	• Student receives vending machine purchase and change from school vending machine	
4. Recognize and request assistance as needed	• Student discusses what to do when vending machine does not give item or provide correct/returned change at school	• Student identifies to adult/peer whom to contact to request assistance in resolving problems when operating vending machine
	• Student role plays actions when machine does not give purchased item or correct/returned change	• Student locates sources for helping to resolve problems when operating vending machines with adult/peer
	• Student identifies whom to request help from in resolving problems when operating vending machine	• Student requests help in resolving a problem when operating vending machines in the community
	• Student role plays locating sources for helping to resolve problems when operating vending machines	
	• Student requests help in resolving a problem operating vending machines	

Domain: Daily Living Skills
Competency 1: Managing Money
Subcompetency 4: Budget Money

Objectives	Training Activities	Home-/Community-Based Training Activities
1. Identify weekly personal income	• Student identifies weekly personal income • Teacher discusses weekly personal income's purpose	• Student identifies earned personal weekly income from job with adult/peer • Adult/peer discusses weekly personal income's use in the community
2. Identify weekly and/or monthly expenses	• Teacher discusses typical weekly and/or monthly expenses • Student identifies typical weekly/monthly expenses • Student makes poster depicting typical weekly/monthly expenses • Student makes chart depicting typical weekly/monthly expenses	• Adult/peer discusses typical weekly and/or monthly expenses • Student determines what her/his weekly/monthly expenses include with adult/peer • Student writes out her/his expenses for a typical week and/or month • Student writes out items that can be purchased with her/his weekly incomes
3. Calculate daily/weekly/monthly expenses	• Teacher demonstrates how to calculate daily/weekly/monthly expenses • Student, using calculator and chart/poster of weekly expenses, figures out personal income and expense budget/total • Student, using calculator and chart/poster of monthly expenses, figures out personal income and expense budget/total • Student seeks assistance from teacher	• Adult/peer demonstrates how to calculate daily/weekly/monthly expenses • Student, using a calculator and written record, figures out weekly personal income and expense budget/total with adult/peer • Student, using a calculator and written record, figures out monthly personal income and expense budget/total with adult/peer • Student seeks assistance from adult/peer
4. Compare expenses to date with remaining personal income	• Teacher demonstrates how to compare expenses to date with remaining personal income • Student keeps records on chart to make weekly comparisons of expenses with remaining income	• Adult demonstrates how to compare expenses to date with remaining personal income • Student keeps her/his own records to make weekly comparison of expenses with remaining income with adult/peer

• Student makes adjustments as needed to not exceed personal income	• Student makes adjustments as needed to not exceed personal income
• Student seeks assistance from teacher	• Student seeks assistance from adult/peer

Domain: Daily Living Skills
Competency 1: Managing Money
Subcompetency 5: Perform Banking Skills

Objectives	Training Activities	Home-/Community-Based Training Activities
1. Open checking account	• Teacher discusses services provided by banks and the benefits of opening and having a checking account • Student visits a local bank and banker discusses the benefits of having a checking account and the various types of checking accounts available • Student knows and can print full name, address, birthdate, telephone number, and names of references • Student practices copying information from ID card to account application for opening a checking account at school bank • Student opens school checking account • Student seeks assistance from teacher	• Student visits a local bank and banker discusses services provided by banks, the benefits of opening and having a checking account, and how to open various types of checking accounts • Student fills out information on account application in order to open a checking account at a bank with adult/peer • Student knows and can print full name, address, birthdate, telephone number, and names of references • Student opens checking account with banker's or adult's/peer's assistance if needed • Student seeks assistance from adult/peer
2. Open savings account	• Teacher discusses services provided by banks and the benefits of opening and having a savings account • Student visits a local bank and banker discusses the benefits of having a savings account • Student practices copying information from ID card to account application for opening a savings account at school bank • Student opens school savings account • Student seeks assistance from teacher	• Student visits a local bank and banker discusses services provided by banks, the benefits of opening and having a savings account, and how to open a savings account • Student fills out information on account application in order to open a savings account at a bank with adult/peer • Student opens savings account with banker's or adult's/peer's assistance if needed • Student seeks assistance from adult/peer
3. Write checks and record transactions	• Teacher demonstrates how to write a check and record transactions in ledger • Student practices writing a check and recording transactions at school bank • Student seeks assistance from teacher	• Adult/peer demonstrates how to write a check and record transactions in ledger • Student writes checks and records transactions for her/his bank checking account with adult/peer • Student seeks assistance from adult/peer
4. Make deposits and record transactions	• Teacher demonstrates how to make deposits and record transactions in ledger for checking and savings accounts • Student practices making deposits and withdrawals and recording transactions at school bank • Student seeks assistance from teacher	• Adult/peer demonstrates how to make deposits and record transactions in ledger for checking and savings accounts • Student makes deposits and withdrawals and records transactions for her/his bank savings accounts • Student seeks assistance from adult/peer
5. Request banking assistance	• Teacher demonstrates how to and with whom to request banking help	• Adult/peer demonstrates how to and with whom to request banking help

DAILY LIVING SKILLS

	• Student demonstrates what to do when problems occur while making checking or savings transactions • Student identifies whom to request help from in resolving problems while making checking or savings transactions • Student role plays actions when problems occur while making checking or savings transactions • Student requests help in resolving problems when making checking or savings transactions	• Student determines when problems occur during checking or savings transactions with adult/peer • Student locates source for requesting help in resolving problems when making checking or savings transactions • Student reviews problem and tries to resolve it himself or herself when making checking or savings transactions • Student requests help in resolving problems when making checking or savings transactions
6. Use check cashing cards/services	• Teacher demonstrates how to use check cashing cards • Student demonstrates the use of check cashing cards/services • Student obtains check cashing cards/services information • Student writes down procedures for using check cashing cards/services on chart/poster • Student verbally explains how to use check cashing cards/services • Student practices using check cashing cards/services • Student demonstrates what to do when problems occur while using check cashing cards/services • Student role plays actions when problems occur while using check cashing cards/services • Student identifies whom to request help from in resolving problems when using check cashing cards/services • Student role plays locating sources for helping to resolve problems when using check cashing cards/services • Student requests help in resolving a problem when using check cashing cards/services • Student seeks assistance from teacher	• Adult/peer demonstrates how to use check cashing cards • Student obtains information for check cashing cards/services with adult/peer • Student obtains check cashing card/service • Student explains how to use check cashing cards/services from procedure in information packets • Student uses check cashing cards/services with adult/peer • Student determines when problems occur while using check cashing cards/services • Student identifies problems in using check cashing cards/services • Student locates sources and requests help in resolving a problem when using check cashing cards/services • Student participates in resolving problem using check cashing cards/services • Student seeks assistance from adult/peer

Domain: Daily Living Skills
Competency 2: Selecting and Maintaining Living Environments
Subcompetency 6: Select Appropriate Community Living Environments

Objectives	Training Activities	Home-/Community-Based Training Activities
1. Identify available living environments	• Teacher discusses various living environments and benefits/disadvantages of each • Student visits living environment options in her/his community	• Adult/peer discusses various living environments and benefits/disadvantages of each • Student visits and discusses available living environments in her/his community
2. Choose appropriate living environments	• Student discusses and lists advantages and disadvantages of each type of living environment in the community	• Student lists advantages and disadvantages of different living environments in her/his community

Objectives	Training Activities	Home-/Community-Based Training Activities
	• Student makes poster of each of the community living environments • Student selects appropriate living environment for her/his needs • Student seeks assistance from teacher	• Student discusses her/his choices of appropriate living environment • Student seeks assistance from adult/peer
3. Identify procedures for renting and connecting utilities	• Teacher describes procedures for renting and connecting utilities • Student visits apartment complex in her/his community, and landlord discusses procedures for renting an apartment and connecting utilities • Student uses ID card to complete apartment application and roll plays telephoning to connect utility companies • Student seeks assistance from teacher	• Adult/peer describes procedures for renting and connecting utilities • Student visits living environment of her/his choice and discusses with landlord the procedures for renting the apartment or house and connecting utilities • Student completes application for lease and telephones the necessary utility companies to connect utilities • Student seeks assistance from adult/peer

Domain: Daily Living Skills
Competency 2: Selecting and Maintaining Living Environments
Subcompetency 7: Maintaining Living Environment

Objectives	Training Activities	Home-/Community-Based Training Activities
1. Identify routine cleaning tasks	• Teacher demonstrates routine cleaning tasks • Student discusses the areas that need to be cleaned weekly • Student visits an apartment/house and discusses with manager the areas that need routine cleaning • Student states what areas of an apartment/house need daily and weekly cleaning • Student demonstrates making and changing bed • Student seeks assistance from teacher	• Adult/peer demonstrates routine cleaning tasks • Student visits an apartment/house and demonstrates which areas need daily or weekly cleaning • Student names with the adult/peer the routine cleaning tasks in the home/apartment that need daily/weekly cleaning • Student identifies what areas of house need daily and weekly cleaning • Student demonstrates making and changing bed • Student seeks assistance from adult/peer
2. Plan daily/weekly cleaning routine	• Student plans approximate time of day for daily cleaning tasks • Student plans tentative day of the week for weekly cleaning tasks • Student develops poster/calendar of daily/weekly cleaning tasks using pictures and/or descriptions • Student seeks assistance from teacher	• Student lists approximate time and plans tentative day of the week for daily or weekly cleaning tasks • Student writes out schedule for day of the week for weekly cleaning tasks • Student develops schedule of daily/weekly cleaning tasks and hangs it up in utility closet • Student seeks assistance from adult/peer
3. Identify and use common household cleaning products	• Teacher demonstrates the common household cleaning products and their uses • Student develops poster/collage of cleaning products for use in daily/weekly cleaning • Student demonstrates the use of each cleaning product • In pairs, students discuss the amounts used in cleaning for each cleaning product on their posters	• Adult/peer demonstrates the common household cleaning products and their uses • Student lists and demonstrates the use of each cleaning product • Student determines the amounts used for each cleaning product • Student performs the cleaning task using the appropriate cleaning product • Student seeks assistance from adult/peer

DAILY LIVING SKILLS

Objectives	Training Activities	Home-/Community-Based Training Activities
	• Student is given cleaning task and performs the task using the appropriate cleaning • Student seeks assistance from teacher	
4. Identify and demonstrate safe use of household cleaning products	• Teacher demonstrates the common household cleaning products and their safe use • Student discusses the dangers of most cleaning products (e.g., to eyes, skin, etc.) • Student demonstrates the use of safety glasses, gloves, aprons, brushes, buckets • Student discusses the precautions listed on all cleaning products • Student states the emergency first aid interventions • Student puts labels on cleaning products, outlining where they should be used (e.g., furniture, bathroom, dishes, countertops, floors, etc.) • Student performs cleaning tasks in school and in community living environments, using cleaning products safely • Student seeks assistance from teacher	• Adult/peer demonstrates the common household cleaning products and their safe use • Student discusses the dangers of most cleaning products, regarding eyes, skin, etc. • Student demonstrates the safe use and the precautions to take when using cleaning products, regarding glasses, gloves, aprons, brushes, buckets, etc. • Student states cleaning products' emergency first aid interventions • Student performs the cleaning task in her/his community living environment, using the cleaning products safely • Student seeks assistance from adult/peer
5. Perform daily/weekly cleaning routine	• Student practices cleaning and charting daily/weekly cleaning tasks • Student seeks assistance from teacher	• Student cleans and charts daily/weekly cleaning tasks at home or in living environment with adult/peer • Student seeks assistance from adult/peer
6. Identify when and where to obtain common household cleaning products	• Teacher discusses when and where to obtain common household cleaning products • Student discusses when to obtain cleaning products • Student discusses where to obtain cleaning products • Student seeks assistance from teacher	• Adult/peer discusses when and where to obtain common household cleaning products • Student demonstrates the appropriate time and place to purchase household cleaning products • Student seeks assistance from adult/peer

Domain: Daily Living Skills
Competency 2: Selecting and Maintaining Living Environments
Subcompetency 8: Use Basic Appliances and Tools

Objectives	Training Activities	Home-/Community-Based Training Activities
1. Identify common household appliances and tools and their uses	• Teacher demonstrates the common household appliances and tools and their uses • Student names common household appliances and tools • Student discusses the uses for the named common household appliances and tools • Student identifies common household appliances and tools appropriate to the cleaning/repair tasks • Student seeks assistance from teacher	• Adult/peer demonstrates the common household appliances and tools and their uses • Student demonstrates the uses for common household appliances and tools • Student identifies the appropriate appliances and tools for the cleaning/repair tasks • Student seeks assistance from adult/peer

Objectives	Training Activities	Home-/Community-Based Training Activities
2. Demonstrate appropriate use of common household appliances and tools	• Teacher describes the common household appliances and tools and their safe use • Student selects on request the appropriate household appliances or tools from the storage area • Student uses common household tools and appliances to perform household cleaning and repair tasks • Student stores tools and appliances in the appropriate area • Student discusses routine care required for tools and appliances • Student seeks assistance from teacher	• Adult/peer describes the common household appliances and tools and their safe use • Student demonstrates the use of common household tools and appliances by performing household cleaning and repair tasks • Student demonstrates storing tools and appliances in the appropriate area • Student demonstrates the required routine care for tools and appliances • Student seeks assistance from adult/peer
3. Identify safety procedures when using household appliances and tools	• Teacher demonstrates the safe use of common household appliances and tools • Student discusses the precautions to be practiced when using common household tools and appliances • Student demonstrates using electrical tools and appliances safely • Student lists "Dos and Don'ts" of using household tools and appliances on chart/poster • Student seeks assistance from teacher	• Adult/peer demonstrates the safe use of common household appliances and tools • Student demonstrates the precautions for using common household tools and appliances • Student demonstrates using electrical tools and appliances safely • Student discusses and lists rules for using household tools and appliances • Student seeks assistance from adult/peer
4. Request appropriate assistance for household repair tasks	• Student demonstrates what to do when faced with household repairs requiring repair person • Student role plays actions when faced with household repairs requiring repair person • Student identifies whom to request help from in resolving repair problems • Student role plays locating sources for help with household repair problems	• Student demonstrates actions when faced with household repairs requiring repair person • Student demonstrates whom to call and locates source in resolving repair problem • Student demonstrates procedure for requesting help in repairing household problem • Student requests help in repairing household problem

Domain: Daily Living Skills
Competency 2: Selecting and Maintaining Living Environments
Subcompetency 9: Set up Personal Living Space

Objectives	Training Activities	Home-/Community-Based Training Activities
1. Identify and select personal living space	• Teacher discusses how to identify and select personal living space • Student names preferred personal living space • Student selects preferred personal living space • Student seeks assistance from teacher	• Adult/peer discusses how to identify and select personal living space • Student selects personal living space • Student seeks assistance from adult/peer
2. Identify and select personal living space furnishings	• Teacher discusses how to identify and select personal living space furnishings	• Adult/peer discusses how to identify and select personal living space furnishings

	• Student discusses different styles of personal living space furnishings • Student names needs for personal living space furnishings • Student develops poster depicting personal living space furnishings • Student seeks assistance from teacher	• Student determines his/her needs for different styles of personal living space furnishings • Student visits stores that provide personal living space furnishings • Student selects personal living space furnishings • Student seeks assistance from adult/peer
3. Arrange personal living space	• Student develops a poster/picture of how personal furnishings will be arranged in preferred personal living space • Student furnishes personal preferred living space at school • Student seeks assistance from teacher	• Student determines and demonstrates how his/her choices of personal furnishings will be arranged in his/her personal living space • Student furnishes personal preferred living space with adult/peer • Student seeks assistance from adult/peer

Domain: Daily Living Skills
Competency 3: Caring for Personal Health
Subcompetency 10: Perform Appropriate Grooming and Hygiene

Objectives	Training Activities	Home-/Community-Based Training Activities
1. Identify grooming products and where to obtain them	• Teacher identifies grooming products and where they can be purchased • Student discusses grooming products he/she should or does use • Student develops poster depicting personal grooming products he/she should or does use • Student discusses retail stores that provide grooming products • Student locates where in the community grooming products can be obtained • Student visits retail store and manager discusses grooming products and costs • Retail store manager discusses, at school, grooming products and costs	• Adult/peer identifies grooming products and where they can be purchased • Student discusses grooming products he/she will or does use • Student locates where in the community grooming products can be obtained • Student visits a retail store and manager discusses grooming products and costs
2. Identify and practice body care skills	• Nurse discusses personal hygiene practices • Nurse discusses menstrual cycle and care skills • Student discusses reasons for showering/bathing daily • Student discusses reasons why there is a need to perform other body hygiene tasks • Student practices shower/bathing skills at school • Student practices other hygiene skills at a community recreational center • Student discusses need for controlling body odor • Student practices controlling body odor • Student demonstrates options for skin care and make-up • Student practices skin care and make-up according to personal preference • Student visits hospital and nurse discusses the need for caring for our bodies and how it relates to good health	• Adult/peer discusses personal hygiene practices • Student discusses reasons for showering/bathing daily • Student demonstrates showering/bathing skills in the community and at home • Student demonstrates other hygiene skills: trimming nails, blowing nose, etc. • Adult/peer discusses menstrual cycle and care skills • Student visits hospital and nurse discusses cleanliness and health issues • Student seeks assistance from adult/peer

Objectives	Training Activities	Home-/Community-Based Training Activities
	• Student develops poster of good hygiene practices • Student seeks assistance from teacher	
3. Identify and practice oral/dental hygiene skills	• Dentist discusses oral/dental hygiene practices • Student discusses the importance of good oral/dental hygiene • Student visits dental office and dentist/hygienist discusses good oral hygiene and demonstrates brushing, flossing, and water picking practices • Student develops poster of good oral hygiene/dental practices • Student seeks assistance from teacher	• Adult/peer discusses oral/dental hygiene practices • Student visits dental office and dental hygienist demonstrates brushing, flossing, and water picking practices • Student demonstrates good oral/dental hygiene • Student seeks assistance from adult/peer
4. Identify and practice hair care skills	• Beautician demonstrates hair care practices • Student discusses the procedures for shampooing and drying hair • Student practices taking care of hair at school and in the community • Student visits hair salon and stylist demonstrates good hair care and styling techniques • Student cuts from fashion magazine hair styles he/she prefers and takes to hair stylist • Student discusses the importance of shaving • Student practices shaving skills • Student practices caring for hair • Student seeks assistance from teacher	• Adult/peer demonstrates hair care practices • Student demonstrates shampooing and drying hair • Student visits hair salon and stylist demonstrates good hair care and styling techniques • Student demonstrates shaving skills • Student demonstrates good hair care • Student seeks assistance from adult/peer
5. Identify and practice toileting skills	• Nurse discusses toileting practices • Student discusses the importance of practicing appropriate toileting skills and washing hands • Student discusses appropriate toileting skills • Student sorts different male and female restroom signs into male and female female stacks • Student operates coin-operated restroom stalls in public restrooms • Student practices toileting skills • Student seeks assistance from teacher	• Adult/peer discusses toileting practices • Student demonstrates appropriate toileting skills • Student demonstrates washing after toileting • Student demonstrates which signs are for male or female restrooms in the community • Student demonstrates correct way to use coin-operated restrooms. • Student demonstrates good toileting skills • Student seeks assistance from adult/peer

Domain: Daily Living Skills
Competency 3: Caring for Personal Health
Subcompetency 11: Dress Appropriately

Objectives	Training Activities	Home-/Community-Based Training Activities
1. Select clothing for different weather conditions	• Teacher discusses dressing for different weather conditions • Student demonstrates what clothing is appropriate for seasonal conditions	• Adult/peer discusses dressing for different weather conditions • Student demonstrates selecting appropriate clothing for seasonal conditions

DAILY LIVING SKILLS

Objectives	Training Activities	Home-/Community-Based Training Activities
	• Student demonstrates storing clothing by season • Student selects and stores clothing for seasons and various weather conditions • Student role plays selecting different clothes for different weather conditions • Student develops poster depicting appropriate clothing for different weather conditions • Student seeks assistance from teacher	• Student demonstrates which clothing to store for the season • Student seeks assistance from adult/peer
2. Select clothing for different activities	• Teacher demonstrates dressing for different daily activities • Student makes poster matching clothing and types of activities • Student selects appropriate clothing for different types of school activities • Student seeks assistance from teacher	• Adult/peer demonstrates dressing for different daily activities • Student demonstrates appropriate clothing for different types of community activities • Student seeks assistance from adult/peer
3. Select and coordinate appropriate fitting clothing	• Teacher demonstrates dressing in coordinated, properly fitting clothing • Student visits retail clothing store, and salesperson discusses the importance of dressing in appropriately sized and coordinated clothing. • Student develops card listing sizes for clothing/shoes/outerwear • Student practices selecting coordinated and fitted clothing for school • Student seeks assistance from teacher	• Adult/peer demonstrates dressing in coordinated, properly fitting clothing • Student visits retail clothing store and salesperson demonstrates coordinated and appropriately sized clothing • Student develops card listing sizes for clothing/shoes/outerwear • Student practices selecting coordinated and fitted clothing for community activities • Student seeks assistance from adult/peer
4. Maintain neat appearance	• Teacher discusses the importance of a neat appearance • Student discusses the importance of a neat appearance at school • Student identifies several times of the day to check and make needed adjustments to appearance at school • Student practices keeping a neat appearance at school • Student seeks assistance from teacher	• Adult/peer discusses the importance of a neat appearance • Student demonstrates that he/she understands the need for keeping a neat appearance in the community • Student demonstrates an overall neat appearance, including hair, teeth, and clothing, in the community • Student practices keeping a neat appearance in the community and at job sites • Student seeks assistance from adult/peer

Domain: Daily Living Skills
Competency 3: Caring for Personal Health
Subcompetency 12: Maintain Physical Fitness

Objectives	Training Activities	Home-/Community-Based Training Activities
1. Identify physical exercises/ activities	• Teacher discusses the importance of exercise and some home examples • Student states physical exercises/activities individual can practice to maintain physical fitness at home	• Adult/peer discusses the importance of exercise and some community examples • Student identifies which physical exercises/ activities individuals can practice to maintain physical fitness in the community

Objectives	Training Activities	Home-/Community-Based Training Activities
	• Student identifies preferred physical home and school exercises/activities • Student seeks assistance from teacher	• Student identifies preferred physical community exercises/activities • Student seeks assistance from adult/peer
2. Practice physical exercises/ activities daily	• Student practices preferred physical exercises/activities daily to maintain adequate fitness level at school/home • Student seeks assistance from teacher	• Student demonstrates the physical exercises/ activities daily and maintains adequate fitness level in the community • Student seeks assistance from adult/peer

Domain: Daily Living Skills
Competency 3: Caring for Personal Health
Subcompetency 13: Recognize and Seek Help for Illness

Objectives	Training Activities	Home-/Community-Based Training Activities
1. Identify signs/symptoms of common illnesses/diseases	• Teacher discusses signs/symptoms of common illnesses/diseases • Student discusses signs/symptoms of common illnesses/diseases • Student role-plays signs/symptoms of common illnesses/diseases • Student seeks assistance from teacher	• Adult/peer discusses signs/symptoms of common illnesses/diseases • Student demonstrates that he/she understands signs/symptoms of common illnesses/diseases • Student seeks assistance from adult/peer
2. Contact medical assistance	• Teacher demonstrates how to contact medical help • Student discusses appropriate medical assistance for common illnesses/diseases • Student role plays contacting appropriate medical assistance for differing identified illnesses/diseases • Student contacts appropriate medical sources when needed • Student practices taking medications safely • Student seeks assistance from teacher	• Adult/peer demonstrates how to contact medical help • Student demonstrates appropriate ways to contact medical assistance for common illnesses/diseases • Student contacts appropriate medical sources when needed • Student practices taking medications safely • Student seeks assistance from adult/peer

Domain: Daily Living Skills
Competency 3: Caring for Personal Health
Subcompetency 14: Practice Basic First Aid

Objectives	Training Activities	Home-/Community-Based Training Activities
1. Perform basic first aid measures	• Nurse describes how to perform basic first aid • Student visits hospital, and nurse demonstrates appropriate basic first aid for minor illnesses/injuries • Student participates in Red Cross basic first aid training • Student role plays basic first aid procedures for minor illnesses/injuries • Student performs first aid procedures for minor illnesses/injuries at school • Nurse discusses need to wear rubber gloves for blood borne pathogens • Student seeks assistance from teacher	• Adult/peer describes how to perform basic first aid • Student visits hospital, and nurse demonstrates appropriate basic first aid for minor illnesses/injuries • Student participates in Red Cross basic first aid training • Student demonstrates first aid procedures for minor illnesses/injuries in the community • Red Cross instructor discusses the need to wear rubber gloves for blood borne pathogens • Student seeks assistance from adult/peer

DAILY LIVING SKILLS

2. Identify emergency situations	• Nurse identifies school/home emergency situations • Student discusses emergency situations • Student visits fire department and firefighter discusses emergency situations (e.g., fire, tornado, hurricane, accident, etc.), appropriate actions to take, and whom to contact • Student makes booklet of school/home/community emergency situations • Student seeks assistance from teacher	• Adult/peer identifies community emergency situations • Student visits fire department and firefighter demonstrates emergency situations (e.g., fire, tornado, hurricane, accident, etc.), appropriate actions to take, and whom to contact • Student seeks assistance from adult/peer
3. Contact emergency assistance	• Teacher demonstrates how to contact emergency help • Student states how and whom to contact for different emergency situations • Student role plays contacting appropriate emergency assistance • Student seeks assistance from teacher	• Adult/peer demonstrates how to contact emergency help • Student demonstrates to adult/peer how and whom to contact for different emergency situations • Student seeks assistance from adult/peer
4. Follow emergency procedures	• Teacher describes emergency procedures at school and home • Student identifies signs identifying emergency assistance and precautions • Student demonstrates appropriate procedures to take during various emergency situations at school or home • Student practices performing appropriate procedures during emergency situations • Student seeks assistance from teacher	• Adult/peer describes emergency procedures in the community or at the job site • Student demonstrates appropriate procedures for various situations in the community or at the job site • Student determines different appropriate procedures for different emergency situations in the community or at the job site with adult/peer • Student practices performing appropriate procedures during emergency situations • Student seeks assistance from adult/peer

Domain: Daily Living Skills
Competency 3: Caring for Personal Health
Subcompetency 15: Practice Personal Safety

Objectives	Training Activities	Home-/Community-Based Training Activities
1. Identify situations that are dangerous in the home, community, and at work	• Teacher describes dangerous situations at school and home • Student discusses situations in the home, community, and at work that require the practicing of personal safety • Student develops poster depicting dangerous situations at school and home • Student seeks assistance from teacher	• Adult/peer describes dangerous situations in the community or at the job site • Student determines situations in the home, community, and at work in which he/she can demonstrate personal safety • Student seeks assistance from adult/peer
2. Identify safety precautions to avoid personal injury in the home, community, and at work	• Teacher describes safety precautions to take at school and home • Student demonstrates safety actions to take to avoid dangerous situations leading to personal injury in the home, community, and at work • Student develops poster depicting safety precautions to take at school and home • Student seeks assistance from teacher	• Adult/peer describes safety precautions to take in the community or at the job site • Student determines safety actions for avoiding dangerous situations that may lead to personal injury in the home, community, and at work • Student seeks assistance from adult/peer

DAILY LIVING SKILLS

3. Identify self-protection procedures	• Police officer describes self-protection procedures to take at school and home • Student demonstrates ways to secure personal living environment • Student visits police station and officer discusses/demonstrates self-protection methods • Student demonstrates ways to protect self when out in public (e.g., traveling in pairs, not hitchhiking, etc.) • Student role plays self-protection procedures to take in school, home, community, and at the job site • Student seeks assistance from teacher	• Adult/peer describes self-protection procedures to take in the community or at the job site • Student visits police station with police officer demonstrating self-protection methods • Student demonstrates different ways to protect self when in community (e.g., travel in groups, be alert) • Student seeks assistance from adult/peer
4. Practice precautions when dealing with strangers	• Officer describes "Dos and Don'ts" when meeting strangers • Student discusses "Dos and Don'ts" of meeting strangers • Student role plays appropriate methods when meeting strangers • Student seeks assistance from teacher	• Adult/peer describes "Dos and Don'ts" of meeting strangers • Student demonstrates appropriate methods of interacting with strangers • Student demonstrates ways to distance self from strangers • Student seeks assistance from adult/peer

Domain: Daily Living Skills
Competency 4: Developing and Maintaining Appropriate Intimate Relationships
Subcompetency 16: Demonstrate Knowledge of Basic Human Sexuality

Objectives	Training Activities	Home-/Community-Based Training Activities
1. Identify basic male and female sexual differences	• Teacher identifies basic differences in males and females and purposes of the differences • Student locates male and female reproductive organs on diagrams or models • Student discusses purpose of the reproductive organs • Student seeks assistance from teacher	• Adult/peer identifies basic differences in males and females and purposes of differences • Student locates male and female reproductive organs on diagrams or models • Student identifies several purposes of the reproductive organs and understands them • Student seeks assistance from adult/peer
2. Describe the human reproduction process	• Student views film/video on human reproduction • Physician discusses the human reproduction process • Student discusses pregnancy and the childbirth stages • Student seeks assistance from teacher	• Student views film/video on human reproduction • Student visits community clinic and physician discusses the human reproduction process • Student demonstrates an understanding of pregnancy and the childbirth stages • Student seeks assistance from adult/peer
3. Discuss personal responsibilities/behaviors	• Teacher identifies basic personal responsibilities/behaviors when expressing human sexuality • Student identifies the reasons for mature human sexual feelings • Student discusses that erections and ejaculations are normal human sexual experiences but are only for private times	• Adult/peer identifies basic personal reponsibilities/behaviors when expressing human sexuality • Student demonstrates an understanding of the reasons for mature human sexual feelings • Student demonstrates an understanding of privacy relating to normal human sexual experiences

	• Student discusses the appropriate times and places for masturbation • Student discusses appropriate sexuality expression with other individuals • Student discusses sexually transmitted diseases and prevention • Student seeks assistance from teacher	• Student identifies an understanding of the appropriate times and places for masturbation • Student discusses appropriate sexuality expression with other individuals • Student discusses sexually transmitted diseases and prevention • Student seeks assistance from adult/peer

Domain: Daily Living Skills
Competency 4: Developing and Maintaining Appropriate Intimate Relationships
Subcompetency 17: Demonstrating Knowledge of Appropriate Dating Behavior

Objectives	Training Activities	Home-/Community-Based Training Activities
1. Identify the physical needs of dating	• Teacher describes the physical needs of dating • Student discusses the need for appropriate touching • Student practices appropriate touching at school and in the community with date • Student seeks assistance from teacher	• Adult/peer describes the physical needs of dating • Student demonstrates an understanding of the need for appropriate touching • Student demonstrates appropriate touching with her/his date • Student seeks assistance from adult/peer
2. Identify the social-emotional needs of dating	• Teacher describes the social-emotional needs of dating • Student discusses the types of relationships (e.g., friends, boyfriend/girlfriend, marriage, etc.) and the mature social-emotional feelings involved in each • Student role plays expressing appropriate feelings for different types of personal relationships • Student practices expressing appropriate feelings for different types of relationships • Student seeks assistance from teacher	• Adult/peer describes the social-emotional needs of dating • Student demonstrates an understanding of types of relationships such as friends, boyfriend/girlfriend, marriage • Student demonstrates the mature social-emotional feelings involved in different types of relationships. • Student demonstrates an understanding of others (different views on relationships) • Student seeks assistance from adult/peer
3. State parents'/guardians' on dating and dating behavior	• Student demonstrates appropriate behavior on a date • Student states parents'/guardians' position on dating and dating behavior • Student seeks assistance from teacher	• Student determines her/his views on appropriate behaviors on a date • Student demonstrates an understanding of others' views on appropriate behaviors on a date • Student seeks assistance from adult/peer

Domain: Daily Living Skills
Competency 5: Eating at Home and in the Community
Subcompetency 18: Plan Balanced Meals

Objectives	Training Activities	Home-/Community-Based Training Activities
1. Identify the basic food groups	• Teacher identifies food guide pyramid • Student names the food guide pyramid groups • Student sorts food products into the food guide pyramid • Student develops poster depicting foods in the food guide pyramid	• Adult/peer identifies food guide pyramid • Student demonstrates understanding of the food guide pyramid by classifying the foods that he/she eats at all three of the meals and at snack times

2. Identify appropriate foods eaten at typical daily meals	• Student states approximate times for meals • Student discusses appropriate foods and portions to be eaten at different meals • Student judges simulated meals as being balanced meals • Student names junk foods and discusses reasons for limiting the amounts consumed	• Student writes out names of foods, determining at which meal they would be served • Student determines which foods are not typical for the different meals • Student demonstrates an understanding of junk foods and healthy foods to adult/peer
3. Plan weekly menu	• Student visits hospital and dietician demonstrates how to plan weekly menu • Student plans weekly word/picture menu • Student seeks assistance from teacher	• Student visits hospital and dietician demonstrates how to plan weekly menu • Student plans a weekly menu including all three meals and snacks • Student seeks assistance from adult/peer

Domain: Daily Living Skills
Competency 5: Eating at Home and in the Community
Subcompetency 19: Purchase Food

Objectives	*Training Activities*	*Home-/Community-Based Training Activities*
1. Construct shopping list from weekly word or picture menu	• Student identifies food products needed to complete a weekly menu • Student develops word/picture shopping list from weekly menu • Student seeks assistance from teacher	• Student makes a list of foods that he/she will need to complete her/his weekly menu • Student develops word/picture shopping list from weekly menu with adult/peer • Student seeks assistance from adult/peer
2. Locate food items on list	• Grocery manager discusses locations of food departments in grocery store • Student visits grocery store and locates foods from shopping list • Student seeks assistance from teacher	• Student demonstrates an understanding of the locations of different food departments in a grocery store • Student locates the groceries he/she needs from his/her shopping list in a grocery store • Student seeks assistance from adult/peer
3. Recognize and request assistance as needed	• Teacher discusses whom to request assistance from in a grocery store • Student discusses whom to request assistance from in a grocery store • Student role plays requesting assistance in a grocery store • Student appropriately requests assistance in a grocery store • Student seeks assistance from teacher	• Adult/peer discusses whom to request assistance from in a grocery store • Student identifies whom to request help from in a grocery store with adult/peer • Student requests assistance in a grocery store • Student seeks assistance from adult/peer
4. Locate cashier	• Student discusses where cashiers are generally located in grocery store • Student demonstrates how to tell whether cashier's lane is open or closed • Student visits grocery store and locates cashier • Student seeks assistance from teacher	• Student locates open cashier's lane in a grocery store • Student demonstrates an understanding of checking out • Student visits grocery store and locates cashier • Student seeks assistance from adult/peer
5. Calculate and give appropriate purchase amount	• Student pays for simulated purchase of groceries from shopping list at school grocery store • Student purchases groceries using the "next dollar" method or writes check for purchase in a grocery store • Student seeks assistance from teacher	• Student demonstrates purchasing groceries using the "next dollar" method or writes check for purchase • Student demonstrates purchases using correct amount • Student seeks assistance from adult/peer

DAILY LIVING SKILLS

6. Receive purchase and change	• Student receives purchase and change for simulated purchase of groceries from shopping list at school grocery store • Student makes purchase and waits for purchase and receives change at grocery store • Student seeks assistance from teacher	• Student receives groceries and correct change from cashier • Student seeks assistance from adult/peer

Domain: Daily Living Skills
Competency 5: Eating at Home and in the Community
Subcompetency 20: Prepare Meals

Objectives	*Training Activities*	*Home-/Community-Based Training Activities*
1. Identify food preparation procedures	• Student visits restaurant and observes food preparation and practices • Student discusses food preparation procedures • Student practices cleaning hands and food preparation area • Student seeks assistance from teacher	• Student visits restaurant, observing food preparation procedures • Student cleans hands and food preparation area • Student seeks assistance from adult/peer
2. Identify and demonstrate uses of basic kitchen tools and appliances	• Teacher discusses basic kitchen tools and appliances and their uses • Student develops poster/collage of kitchen tools and appliances and their uses • Student visits restaurant and chef discusses and demonstrates the uses of basic food preparation tools and appliances • Student names basic kitchen tools and appliances • Student demonstrates the safety precautions when using basic kitchen tools and appliances • Student practices using basic kitchen tools and appliances • Student seeks assistance from teacher	• Adult/peer discusses basic kitchen tools and appliances and their uses • Student lists and discusses the use of each kitchen tool and appliance • Student visits restaurant and chef demonstrates food preparation and use of kitchen tools and appliances • Student demonstrates familiarity with basic kitchen tools and appliances, and safety precautions, with adult/peer • Student use basic kitchen tools and appliances safely • Student seeks assistance from adult/peer
3. Select recipe	• Student practices selecting appropriate recipes for meals • Student seeks assistance from teacher	• Student selects appropriate recipes for meals • Student seeks assistance from adult/peer
4. Collect foods and utensils listed on recipe	• Student practices collecting food products and cooking utensils needed to follow recipes • Student seeks assistance from teacher	• Student collects food products and cooking utensils needed for following recipe • Student seeks assistance from adult/peer

5. Follow simple recipe	• Student visits restaurant and chef demonstrates how to follow simple recipe for preparing a meal
	• Student follows simple no-cook recipe
	• Student follows simple cook recipe
	• Student demonstrates how to use microwave to follow recipe
	• Student follows microwave recipe
	• Student follows oven/stove recipe
	• Student discusses signs of overcooked foods
	• Student seeks assistance from teacher
		• Student visits a restaurant, with chef preparing a simple meal from a recipe
		• Student prepares from recipes:
		  a. no-cook meal
		  b. toaster, no-cook recipes
		  c. microwave recipe
		  d. oven-/stove-cooked recipe
		• Student points out overcooked meal and discusses signs of overcooked foods
		• Student seeks assistance from adult/peer

Domain: Daily Living Skills
Competency 5: Eating at Home and in the Community
Subcompetency 21: Demonstrate Appropriate Eating Habits

Objectives	Training Activities	Home-/Community-Based Training Activities
1. Demonstrate table setting	• Teacher demonstrates appropriate table settings • Student demonstrates procedures for setting table • Student makes poster of appropriate place setting for table setting • Student practices setting the table for meals • Student seeks assistance from adult/peer	• Adult/peer demonstrates appropriate table settings • Student demonstrates appropriate way of setting the table for meals with adult/peer • Student seeks assistance from adult/peer
2. Demonstrate appropriate serving of food	• Teacher demonstrates appropriate serving of food • Student demonstrates procedures for serving foods • Student practices appropriate way to serve food • Student seeks assistance from teacher	• Adult/peer demonstrates appropriate serving of food • Student demonstrates appropriate way to serve food • Student seeks assistance from adult/peer
3. Demonstrate appropriate eating manners	• Teacher demonstrates appropriate eating habits • Student demonstrates eating etiquette • Student practices appropriate eating manners • Student seeks assistance from teacher	• Adult/peer demonstrates appropriate eating habits • Student demonstrates understanding of appropriate eating manners • Student seeks assistance from adult/peer

Domain: Daily Living Skills
Competency 5: Eating at Home and in the Community
Subcompetency 22: Demonstrate Meal Clean-Up and Food Storage

Objectives	Training Activities	Home-/Community-Based Training Activities
1. Demonstrate meal clean-up procedures	• Teacher demonstrates appropriate meal clean-up procedures • Student discusses the importance of meal clean-up immediately after mealtime • Student demonstrates the procedure for meal clean-up • Student practices removing leftover food from table • Student practices removing dishes from table • Student practices cleaning the table of food scraps and crumbs • Student demonstrates the procedures for washing, drying, and storing clean dishes • Student practices the procedures for washing, drying, and storing clean dishes • Student inspects eating area after meal clean-up • Student seeks assistance from teacher	• Adult/peer demonstrates appropriate meal clean-up procedures • Student identifies the importance of meal clean-up • Student removes leftover food from table • Student removes dishes from table • Student uses space to clean the table of food scraps and crumbs • Student washes, dries, and stores clean dishes • Student reviews eating area after meal clean-up and repeats any necessary procedures • Student seeks assistance from adult/peer

DAILY LIVING SKILLS

2. Identify signs of food spoilage	• Teacher describes signs of food spoilage • Student discusses the signs of food spoilage • Student discusses the consequences of eating spoiled foods • Student finds spoiled foods in a group of foods • Student seeks assistance from teacher	• Adult/peer describes signs of food spoilage • Student demonstrates an understanding of food spoilage and includes the signs and consequences • Student seeks assistance from adult/peer
3. Demonstrate waste disposal procedures	• Teacher demonstrates waste disposal procedures • Student discusses reasons for proper waste disposal • Student demonstrates procedures for using and cleaning trash receptacles • Student observes school cook using the garbage disposal • Student demonstrates the appropriate use of garbage disposal • Student demonstrates the appropriate methods of disposing of food waste • Student seeks assistance from teacher	• Adult/peer demonstrates waste disposal procedures • Student demonstrates an understanding of the reasons for disposing of food wastes and trash preparation • Student demonstrates that he/she understands the procedures for using and cleaning trash receptacles and garbage disposals • Student demonstrates the appropriate ways to dispose of food and use garbage disposals • Student seeks assistance from adult/peer
4. Sort food into storage groups	• Student observes school cook placing food in appropriate containers and wrapping foods • Student practices wrapping foods to be stored • Student practices placing foods in containers to be stored • Student practices checking food for spoilage weekly • Student practices appropriate food storage • Student seeks assistance from teacher	• Student demonstrates which foods can be wrapped and which foods can be placed in containers for storing • Student demonstrates that he/she understands how to check food for spoilage • Student stores food appropriately in a kitchen after visit to a grocery store • Student seeks assistance from adult/peer
5. Demonstrate appropriate food storage	• Student visits restaurant and chef demonstrates food storage into appropriate groups • Student discusses why foods are stored in different locations • Student develops posters depicting foods stored in refrigerator, in cool places, pantries, etc. • Student sorts and stores food in the school food preparation/storage area for school cooks • Student seeks assistance from teacher	• Student learns how to store food into appropriate groups by visiting restaurant • Student writes out where food is stored in kitchen • Student stores food in his/her own living space • Student seeks assistance from adult/peer

Domain: Daily Living Skills
Competency 5: Eating at Home and in the Community
Subcompetency 23: Demonstrate Appropriate Restaurant Dining

Objectives	Training Activities	Home-/Community-Based Training Activities
1. Identify types of restaurants	• Teacher describes different types of restaurants • Student develops a poster depicting types of restaurants • Student discusses different types of restaurants	• Adult/peer describes different types of restaurants • Student writes out the different types of restaurants

2. Estimate meal costs and bring sufficient money to dine out	• Student discusses where he/she is to dine out • Student estimates meal costs • Student secures estimated money to cover meal costs prior to dining out • Student seeks assistance from teacher	• Student estimates restaurants that he/she has enough money to dine in • Student estimates what food he/she can have for meal with his/her given supply of money • Student seeks assistance from adult/peer
3. Order from wall/printed menus	• Student role plays ordering meal from wall/printed menus from different types of restaurants • Student orders meals from wall/printed menus	• Student orders meals from wall/printed menus in various restaurants
4. Demonstrate eating manners	• Teacher demonstrates appropriate eating-out habits • Student demonstrates appropriate eating manners when dining out • Student practices appropriate eating manners when dining out	• Adult/peer demonstrates appropriate eating-out habits • Student demonstrates he/she understands appropriate eating manners when dining out
5. Pay bill and tip appropriately	• Student discusses various ways to pay for restaurant meals (pay cashier or waiter) • Student discusses the types of restaurants that accept only currency or checks • Student discusses tipping policies • Student role plays paying meal bills and tipping • Student practices paying meal bills and tipping	• Student demonstrates various ways for paying for food in a restaurant (check, currency, credit card) • Student demonstrates appropriate amount to tip, and in which restaurants not to tip • Student demonstrates how he/she would pay her/his bill and tip in a restaurant

Domain: Daily Living Skills
Competency 6: Cleaning and Purchasing Clothing
Subcompetency 24: Wash/Dry Clothes

Objectives	Training Activities	Home-/Community-Based Training Activities
1. Identify types and uses of laundry products	• Teacher describes types and uses of laundry products • Student visits home economics teacher, and she discusses and demonstrates the use of laundry products (e.g., detergents, bleaches, spot prewashes, softeners, and dryer sheets) • Student develops poster with laundry products • Student discusses the types and uses of each type of laundry product • Student seeks assistance from teacher	• Adult/peer describes types and uses of laundry products • Student demonstrates the use of laundry products such as detergents, bleaches, spot prewashes, softeners, dryer sheets • Student seeks assistance from adult/peer
2. Sort clothing by temperature, load, and colors	• Teacher demonstrates sorting clothes by temperature, load, and colors • Student locates temperature and load settings on school/home washing machine • Student demonstrates how clothes should be sorted for washing and the reasons to do this • Student sorts clothing appropriately • Student seeks assistance from teacher	• Adult/peer demonstrates sorting clothes by temperature, load, and colors • Student locates temperature and load settings on washing machine • Student sorts clothes appropriately • Student seeks assistance from adult/peer

DAILY LIVING SKILLS

3. Load clothes

- Student visits home economics teacher, who demonstrates how to wash/dry clothes
- Student practices loading clothing in school/home washing machine
- Student seeks assistance from teacher

- Student demonstrates appropriate way to load clothes into washer/dryer
- Student loads clothes in washing machine
- Student seeks assistance from adult/peer

4. Add detergent

- Student visits home economics teacher, who demonstrates how to wash/dry clothes
- Student practices adding detergent
- Student seeks assistance from teacher

- Student demonstrates appropriate amount and type of detergent to add to clothes in washing machine
- Student adds detergent in washing machine
- Student seeks assistance from adult/peer

5. Set temperature and load settings

- Student visits home economics teacher, who demonstrates how to wash/dry clothes
- Student practices setting the load temperature and load settings
- Student seeks assistance from teacher

- Student demonstrates appropriate way to set the temperature and water amount on washing machine
- Student demonstrates settings with different loads with adult/peer
- Student seeks assistance from adult/peer

6. Start washing machine

- Student visits home economics teacher, who demonstrates how to wash/dry clothes
- Student practices starting washing machine
- Student seeks assistance from teacher

- Student demonstrates how to start washing machine
- Student demonstrates starting washing machine with adult/peer
- Student seeks assistance from adult/peer

7. Remove clothes at end of washing cycle and hang non-dryable clothes up to dry

- Student visits home economics teacher, who demonstrates how to wash/dry clothes
- Student practices removing clothes at end of the washing cycle and hanging non-dryable clothes up to dry
- Student seeks assistance from teacher

- Student removes clothing from washing machine when machine stops and hangs nondryable clothes up to dry
- Student hangs nondryable clothes on line to dry
- Student seeks assistance from adult/peer

8. Load washed clothes in dryer

- Student visits home economics teacher, who demonstrates how to wash/dry clothes
- Student practices loading washed clothes in dryer
- Student seeks assistance from teacher

- Student demonstrates loading clothes into dryer with adult/peer
- Student loads clothes in dryer with adult/peer
- Student seeks assistance from adult/peer

9. Set temperature and time dials

- Student visits home economics teacher, who demonstrates how to wash/dry clothes
- Student practices setting temperature and time dials
- Student seeks assistance from teacher

- Student sets temperature and time dials appropriately for the load
- Student sets temperature and time dials with adult/peer
- Student seeks assistance from adult/peer

10. Start dryer

- Student visits home economics teacher, who demonstrates how to wash/dry clothes
- Student practices starting dryer
- Student seeks assistance from teacher

- Student demonstrates how to start dryer
- Student starts dryer with adult/peer
- Student seeks assistance from adult/peer

11. Remove clothes from dryer and hang or fold at end of drying cycle

- Student visits home economics teacher, who demonstrates how to wash/dry clothes
- Student practices removing clothes from dryer and hanging or folding at end of drying cycle
- Student demonstrates how to iron wrinkled clothes
- Student seeks assistance from teacher

- Student removes clothing from dryer and hangs or folds when clothes are dry
- Student hangs clothes on hanger or folds when dry from dryer with adult/peer
- Student demonstrates how to iron wrinkled clothes
- Student seeks assistance from adult/peer

12. Store clothes	• Student demonstrates how and where clothes should be stored • Student practices storing clothes • Student seeks assistance from teacher	• Student demonstrates an understanding of storing clothes • Student puts clothes away after drying with adult/peer • Student seeks assistance from adult/peer
13. Perform minor maintenance procedures	• Student visits home appliance retail store and manager discusses minor maintenance practices on appliances • Student performs minor maintenance on washing machines and dryers • Student seeks assistance from teacher	• Student demonstrates an understanding of minor maintenance on washer and dryer • Student performs routine maintenance on washer and dryer with adult/peer • Student seeks assistance from adult/peer
14. Perform washing/drying clothes at laundromat	• Student visits laundromat and attendant demonstrates using washing machines and dryers • Student washes and dries clothes at laundromat • Student requests assistance from laundromat attendant	• Student visits laundromats and demonstrates skills of washing/drying clothes, using coin-operated machines. • Student demonstrates requesting assistance from attendant

Domain: Daily Living Skills
Competency 6: Cleaning and Purchasing Clothing
Subcompetency 25: Buy Clothes

Objectives	Training Activities	Home-/Community-Based Training Activities
1. Identify basic clothing needs	• Student visits clothing store and salesperson discusses a basic wardrobe • Student discusses number and types of clothes needed to compose a wardrobe • Student develops a poster depicting basic clothing needed for wardrobe	• Student visits clothing store and demonstrates knowledge of basic clothes needed to compose a wardrobe
2. Identify appropriate size, color, and style of clothing needed	• Student discusses the size, color, and style of clothes he/she needs for a wardrobe • Student seeks assistance from teacher	• Student demonstrates knowledge of the size, color, and style of clothes needed for wardrobe • Student seeks assistance from adult/peer
3. Estimate clothing costs and bring money for clothing needs	• Student identifies current clothing needs • Student estimates costs for clothing needs and brings amount to make needed purchases	• Student demonstrates knowledge of costs for clothing needs • Student brings amount needed to make purchases
4. Identify appropriate clothing store	• Student discusses appropriate types of clothing stores to shop at • Student seeks assistance from teacher	• Student identifies appropriate store to shop at for clothing • Student seeks assistance from adult/peer
5. Locate appropriate store department	• Student states the location of clothing store departments • Student locates appropriate clothing departments • Student seeks assistance from teacher	• Student approriately locates which clothing department to shop in for each item • Student seeks assistance from adult/peer
6. Request assistance from store clerk	• Student role plays asking store clerk for assistance • Student identifies the school store clerks • Student requests assistance from school store clerk	• Student identifies store clerks and appropriately requests information from them

7. Select clothing item(s)	• Student develops poster of clothing needs • Student selects clothing item(s) • Student seeks assistance from teacher	• Student selects appropriate clothing item(s) • Student selects, from catalogs, appropriate clothes with adult/peer • Student seeks assistance from adult/peer
8. Check fit of clothing item(s)	• Sales clerk discusses clothing sizing • Student discusses how to check clothing fit • Student checks fit of clothing prior to purchasing • Student seeks assistance from teacher	• Adult/peer discusses clothing sizing • Student checks fit of clothing item • Student demonstrates appropriate way to request assistance from sales clerk • Student seeks assistance from adult/peer
9. Locate cashier	• Student demonstrates where cashiers are generally located in clothing stores • Student locates cashier to make purchase of clothes • Student seeks assistance from teacher	• Student locates cashier to purchase clothing • Student tells adult/peer where to find cashiers in clothing stores • Student seeks assistance from adult/peer
10. Calculate and give appropriate purchase amount	• Student role plays the calculating and use of the "next dollar" method to pay for simulated purchase and make purchase • Student uses "next dollar" method to pay for clothing purchase and make purchase • Student seeks assistance from teacher	• Student uses "next dollar" method to pay for purchases • Student uses correct amount of money to pay for purchases • Student seeks assistance from adult/peer
11. Receive purchase and change	• Student role plays receiving purchase and change • Student receives purchase and change • Student seeks assistance from teacher	• Student receives purchase and determines whether he/she should receive change • Student receives purchase and change with adult/peer • Student seeks assistance from adult/peer

Domain: Daily Living Skills
Competency 7: Participate in Leisure/Recreational Activities
Subcompetency 26: Identify Available Community Leisure/Recreational Activities

Objectives	Training Activities	Home-/Community-Based Training Activities
1. Identify types of individual leisure/recreational activities	• Student discusses the importance of participating in individual leisure/recreational activities • Student visits YMCA/YWCA or community recreational center and director discusses and demonstrates activities that can be performed alone during leisure time • Student demonstrates various activities that an individual can perform alone during leisure time • Student develops posters depicting activities he/she enjoys performing alone during leisure time • Student seeks assistance from teacher	• Student visits YMCA/YWCA or community recreational center and watches others participate in activities that can be performed alone during leisure time • Student visits YMCA/YWCA or community recreational center and participates in activities that can be performed alone during leisure time • Student seeks assistance from adult/peer

2. Identify types of group leisure/ recreational activities	• Student discusses the importance of participating in group leisure/recreational activities • Student visits YMCA/YWCA or community recreational center and director discusses and demonstrates activities that can be performed in a group during leisure time • Student demonstrates various activities that an individual can perform in a group during leisure time • Student develops posters depicting activities he/she enjoys performing in a group during during leisure time • Student seeks assistance from teacher	• Student visits YMCA/YWCA or community recreational center and watches others participate in activities that can be performed in a group during leisure time • Student visits YMCA/YWCA or community recreational center and participates in activities that can be performed in a group during leisure time • Student seeks assistance from adult/peer
3. Locate equipment and facilities of leisure/recreational activities	• Student visits YMCA/YWCA or community recreational center and director discusses where equipment and facilities can be found for participating in leisure/recreational activities • Student locates where equipment and facilities for leisure/recreational activities can be found • Student locates the sources for assisting in identifying leisure/recreational activities in the community using telephone directory • Student seeks assistance from teacher	• Student visits YMCA/YWCA or recreational center in community and locates where equipment and facilities for leisure/recreational activities can be found • Student visits YMCA/YWCA or recreational center in community and locates where the sources for assisting in identifying leisure/recreational activities can be found • Student seeks assistance from adult/peer

Domain: Daily Living Skills
Competency 7: Participate in Leisure/Recreational Activities
Subcompetency 27: Select and Plan Leisure/Recreational Activities

Objectives	Training Activities	Home-/Community-Based Training Activities
1. Identify personal leisure/ recreational activities and interests	• Recreational director discusses the availability of leisure/recreational activities in the community • Student identifies personal leisure/recreational activities and interests • Student states preference for personal community leisure/recreational activities and interests • Student states preference for personal home leisure/recreational activities and interests • Student seeks assistance from teacher	• Adult/peer discusses the availability of leisure/recreational activities in the community and visits community center with student • Student makes a list of personal community leisure/recreational activities and interests • Student discusses and states preference for personal leisure/recreational activities and interests • Student states preference for personal home leisure/recreational activities and interests • Student seeks assistance from adult/peer
2. Identify costs, time, and physical requirements of leisure/recreational activities	• Recreational director discusses the costs, time, and physical requirements of leisure/recreational activities in the community • Student discusses the costs, time, and physical requirements of leisure/recreational activities depicted on her/his poster • Student seeks assistance from teacher	• Adult/peer discusses the costs, time, and physical requirements of leisure/recreational activities in the community • Student writes out on lists the costs, time, and physical requirements of leisure/recreational activities and interests • Student seeks assistance from adult/peer

DAILY LIVING SKILLS

3. Develop weekly schedule of leisure/recreational activities	• Recreational director demonstrates how to construct a weekly schedule of leisure/recreational activities • Student constructs personal word/picture/symbol charts of weekly schedule of leisure/recreational activities • Student seeks assistance from teacher	• Adult/peer demonstrates how to construct a weekly schedule of leisure/recreational activities • Student writes out personal charts of weekly schedule of leisure/recreational activities and interests, which may contain pictures or symbols • Student seeks assistance from adult/peer

Domain: Daily Living Skills
Competency 7: Participate in Leisure/Recreational Activities
Subcompetency 28: Participate in Individual and Group Leisure/Recreational Activities

Objectives	Training Activities	Home-/Community-Based Training Activities
1. Identify and obtain necessary equipment	• P.E. teacher identifies and discusses how to obtain leisure/recreational equipment • Student states equipment needed for preferred leisure activities • Student practices purchasing, borrowing, and renting equipment needed for preferred leisure activities • Student seeks assistance from teacher	• Adult/peer identifies and discusses how to obtain leisure/recreational equipment • Student visits shops that stock equipment needed for preferred leisure activities • Student rents or purchases some equipment needed for preferred leisure activities • Student seeks assistance from adult/peer
2. Identify and follow rules of leisure/recreational activities	• P.E. teacher identifies and discusses how to follow rules of leisure/recreational activities • Student discusses the rules in her/his preferred leisure/recreational activities • Student practices following rules and safety precautions in preferred leisure/recreational activities • Student seeks assistance from teacher	• Adult/peer identifies and discusses how to follow rules of leisure/recreational activities • Student demonstrates an understanding of rules and safety precautions in preferred leisure/recreational activities • Student seeks assistance from adult/peer

Domain: Daily Living Skills
Competency 7: Participate in Leisure/Recreational Activities
Subcompetency 29: Select and Participate in Group Travel

Objectives	Training Activities	Home-/Community-Based Training Activities
1. Identify travel interests	• Travel agent discusses travel/vacation options • Student visits travel agency and travel agent discusses travel options and procedures • Student discusses travel/vacation interests • Student constructs a poster depicting travel/vacation interests	• Adult/peer discusses travel/vacation options • Student visits travel agency and explores interests with travel agent for travel or vacations • Student writes out a list of travel/vacation interests
2. Identify travel possibilities	• Travel agent discusses travel/vacation options • Student states travel possibilities within time and costs framework, with assistance	• Adult/peer discusses travel/vacation options • Student determines travel possibilities within time and costs framework, using assistance if needed
3. Identify expenses and resources needed for travel	• Travel agent discusses expenses and resources needed for travel/vacation	• Adult/peer discusses expenses and resources needed for travel/vacation

	• Student, with assistance, identifies costs and needed resources for travel plans • Student seeks assistance from teacher	• Student writes out a list of travel plans, determining costs and needed resources • Student seeks assistance from adult/peer
4. Request assistance in travel planning	• Student seeks assistance in planning travel • Student develops chart listing resources for assisting in setting up vacation/travel, also including telephone numbers and contacts	• Student demonstrates an understanding of where to seek assistance in planning travel • Student develops listing of resources for assisting in setting up vacation/travel, also including telephone numbers and contacts
5. Demonstrate appropriate travel behavior	• Student demonstrates appropriate behavior when traveling in group or individual travel in various modes of transportation	• Student demonstrates appropriate behavior when traveling in group or individual travel in various modes of transportation

Domain: Daily Living Skills
Competency 8: Getting Around in the Community
Subcompetency 30: Follow Traffic Rules and Safety Procedures

Objectives	Training Activities	Home-/Community-Based Training Activities
1. Identify common traffic and safety signs and rules	• Student visits the police department and police officer discusses the community's traffic signs and rules to follow • Student travels around the community and lists the common traffic and safety signs and rules in the community • Student seeks assistance from teacher	• Student visits the police department and police officer discusses the community's traffic signs and rules to follow • Student travels around the community and demonstrates an understanding of common traffic and safety signs and rules in the community • Student seeks assistance from adult/peer
2. Practice following common traffic and safety signs and rules	• Student demonstrates following common traffic signs and rules on the way to school and keeps journal of successes • Student seeks assistance from teacher	• Student demonstrates other safety precautions he/she can use while on city streets, other than traffic rules • Student seeks assistance from adult/peer

Domain: Daily Living Skills
Competency 8: Getting Around in the Community
Subcompetency 31: Develop and Follow Community Access Routes

Objectives	Training Activities	Home-/Community-Based Training Activities
1. Identify routinely used community locations	• Student identifies community locations routinely traveled to and lists on chart • Student discusses routinely utilized community locations • Student develops collage with picture, handouts, brochures of visited community locations for a week • Student seeks assistance from teacher	• Student writes out a list of places traveled to in a week with adult/peer • Adult/peer discusses community locations routinely traveled to • Student seeks assistance from adult/peer • Student visits bus company and personnel explain commonly utilized routes for community trips
2. Plan and practice following important community routes	• Bus/taxi company representative discusses important community routes • Student states routes to several locations listed on collage of important community routes	• Adult/peer discusses important community routes • Student demonstrates an understanding of important community routes by major mode of relevant transportation

DAILY LIVING SKILLS

	• Student practices following important routes by major mode of transportation • Student seeks assistance from teacher	• Student practices following important routes by major mode of transportation • Student seeks assistance from adult/peer
3. Request assistance as needed	• Student identifies sources for providing assistance in accessing important community locations • Student requests appropriate assistance for community access	• Student demonstrates an understanding of requesting appropriate assistance for community access • Student requests appropriate assistance for community access

Domain: Daily Living Skills
Competency 8: Getting Around in the Community
Subcompetency 32: Access Available Transportation

Objectives	Training Activities	Home-/Community-Based Training Activities
1. Identify modes of transportation in the community	• Student visits local bus or taxicab company in town and dispatcher discusses and demonstrates how to use local modes of transportation in the community • Student discusses the modes of available transportation in the community • Student states her/his types of personal transportation	• Student visits local bus and taxicab company in town, demonstrating an understanding of the use of local modes of transportation in the community • Student identifies her/his preference for available transportation in the community
2. Identify requirements of each mode of community transportation	• Student visits local bus or taxicab company in town and dispatcher discusses the requirements for using each community mode of transportation • Student states the requirements for using her/his major mode of transportation • Student seeks assistance from teacher	• Student demonstrates an understanding of the requirements for using each community mode of transportation • Student states the requirements for using her/his major mode of transportation with adult/peer • Student seeks assistance from adult/peer
3. Practice using modes of community transportation	• Student practices using the various types of community transportation • Student participates in bike safety training program • Student participates in public transportation training program • Student seeks assistance from teacher	• Student demonstrates that he/she can use the various types of community transportation independently • Student participates in bike safety training program • Student uses or demonstrates an understanding of curb-to-curb van service • Student seeks assistance from adult/peer
4. Request assistance for using modes of community transportation	• Student identifies sources of assistance for travel in the community for any of the available modes of transportation and lists on chart/poster • Student requests assistance from appropriate sources for using modes of community travel	• Student demonstrates an understanding of requesting assistance for any of the available modes of transportation in the community to adult/peer • Student requests assistance from appropriate sources for using modes of community travel
5. Identify and develop strategies for coping with disruption in primary community transportation mode	• Teacher demonstrates strategies to use when there is a disruption in primary transportation	• Adult/peer demonstrates strategies to use when there is a disruption in primary transportation

• Student discusses her/his options for use of community travel when major mode is disrupted • Student states her/his strategies for using alternative modes of transportation when primary mode is disrupted • Student seeks assistance from teacher	• Student determines which other modes of transportation she/he can use when her/his major mode is disrupted • Student explores ways of travel when all of her/his primary modes of transportation are disrupted • Student seeks assistance from adult/peer

PERSONAL-SOCIAL SKILLS

Domain: Personal-Social Skills
Competency 9: Acquiring Self-Identity
Subcompetency 33: Demonstrate Knowledge of Personal Interests

Objectives	Training Activities	Home-/Community-Based Training Activities
1. Identify and describe personal interests	• Teacher discusses why people have interests and examples of interests • Student discusses personal interests with her/his parents and siblings • Student constructs poster outlining some of her/his personal interests • Student seeks assistance from teacher	• Adult/peer describes her/his personal interests and examples of other people's interests • Adult/peer explains how her/his personal interests were developed • Adult/peer explores the community with student, discussing other peoples' personal interests/abilities • Student seeks assistance from adult/peer
2. Identify and describe personal abilities	• Teacher discusses why people have abilities and examples of abilities • Student discusses and defines personal abilities • Student discusses personal abilities with her/his parents and siblings • Student constructs poster outlining her/his personal abilities • Student seeks assistance from teacher	• Adult/peer describes her/his personal abilities and examples of other people's abilities • Student describes her/his personal abilities • Student explains the development of her/his personal abilities • Student explores other people's abilities in the community • Student seeks assistance from adult/peer

Domain: Personal-Social Skills
Competency 9: Acquiring Self Identity
Subcompetency 34: Demonstrate Appropriate Responses to Emotions

Objectives	Training Activities	Home-/Community-Based Training Activities
1. Identify different emotions	• Teacher discusses why people have emotions and examples of emotions • Student names common emotions that people express • Student develops list and teacher lists on chart or chalkboard several common emotions expressed daily • Student develops poster by cutting and pasting pictures from magazines of people demonstrating the emotions listed on chart or chalkboard • Student seeks assistance from teacher	• Adult/peer describes her/his personal emotions and examples of other people's emotions • Student demonstrates an understanding of emotions that people express • Student identifies emotions from pictures of people in magazines and newspapers • Student seeks assistance from adult/peer

PERSONAL-SOCIAL SKILLS

PERSONAL-SOCIAL SKILLS

2. Identify ways to express emotions	• Teacher discusses ways people can express and examples of emotions • Student demonstrates ways emotions listed on the chart or chalkboard are expressed • Student role plays expressing emotions listed on chart or chalkboard • Student seeks assistance from teacher	• Adult/peer describes how he/she expresses emotions and examples of how other people express emotions • Student identifies emotions expressed by other adult peers in work settings or in the community to adult/peer • Student seeks assistance from adult/peer
3. Practice appropriate ways to express emotions	• Student states emotions that are difficult for him/her to express and role plays strategies to express them appropriately • Student develops self-monitoring plan for tracking difficult-to-express emotions • Student demonstrates appropriate ways to express emotions • Student seeks assistance from teacher	• Student describes which emotions are hard for him/her to express in work settings and in the community • Student explains these difficult emotions he/she sees with other adult peers in work settings and in the community • Student demonstrates appropriate ways to express those difficult emotions in work settings and in the community • Student seeks assistance from adult/peer
4. Request assistance for coping with emotions	• Student identifies sources of assistance for coping with emotions and lists telephone numbers and contacts on chart/poster • Student role plays seeking assistance for coping with emotions • Student requests assistance to help him/her cope with emotions	• Student demonstrates an understanding of how to request assistance in coping with her/his difficult emotions in work settings and in the community to adult/peer • Student requests assistance from adult/peer for coping with emotions

Domain: Personal-Social Skills
Competency 9: Acquiring Self-Identity
Subcompetency 35: Display Self-Confidence and Self-Worth

Objectives	Training Activities	Home-/Community-Based Training Activities
1. Identify positive aspects of people in general	• Counselor discusses positive aspects of people in general • Student discusses common positive personal behaviors people exhibit • Student names common positive personal behaviors that people exhibit • Student develops list and teacher lists on chart or chalkboard several common personal positive behaviors that people exhibit daily • Student develops poster by cutting and pasting pictures from magazines of people demonstrating common positive personal behaviors listed on chart or chalkboard	• Adult/peer discusses positive aspects of people in general • Student discusses common positive personal work and community behaviors • Student demonstrates an understanding of positive personal work and community behaviors • Student identifies positive personal work behaviors from pictures of people in magazines and newspapers
2. Identify positive aspects of self	• Student identifies common positive personal behaviors • Student names 5 common positive personal behaviors that he/she exhibits • Student develops list and teacher lists on chart or chalkboard several common personal positive behaviors he/she exhibits daily	• Student demonstrates common positive personal work and community behaviors • Student names 5 common critical statements expressed in the work settings and in the community • Student identifies positive personal work behaviors he/she should exhibit from pictures in magazines and newspapers

	• Student develops poster by cutting and pasting pictures from magazines of people demonstrating his/her common positive personal behaviors listed on chart or chalkboard	
3. Practice displaying self-confidence and self-worth	• Student identifies behaviors of self-confidence and self-worth that are difficult for him/her to exhibit • Student develops self-monitoring plan for tracking difficult-to-exhibit behaviors of self-confidence and self-worth • Student demonstrates appropriate self-confidence and self-worth in role-play scenarios • Student demonstrates examples of self-confidence and self-worth in the classroom	• Student describes which behaviors of self-confidence and self-worth in the work setting and in the community are difficult to exhibit • Student explains these difficult-to-exhibit behaviors of self-confidence and self-worth to training program supervisor, job placement supervisor, or adults in the community • Student demonstrates appropriate ways to express self-confidence and self-worth with training program or job placement supervisor and in the community • Student demonstrates examples of appropriate self-confidence and self-worth in training programs and job placements and in the community

Domain: Personal-Social Skills
Competency 9: Acquiring Self-Identity
Subcompetency 36: Demonstrating Giving and Accepting Praise and Criticism

Objectives	Training Activities	Home-/Community-Based Training Activities
1. Identify statements of praise	• Counselor discusses statements of praise that people express • Student identifies common statements of praise that people express • Student names 5 common statements of praise that people express • Student develops list and teacher lists on chart or chalkboard several common statements of praise daily • Student develops poster by cutting and pasting statements of praise listed in magazines and newspapers from the chart or chalkboard lists • Student seeks assistance from teacher	• Adult/peer discusses statements of praise that people express • Student identifies common statements of praise expressed in work settings and in the community • Student names 5 common statements of praise expressed in work settings and in the community • Student identifies statements of praise expressed in work settings or in the community listed in magazines or "world of work" textbooks and newspaper • Student seeks assistance from adult/peer
2. Identify appropriate/inappropriate responses to praise	• Counselor discusses appropriate/inappropriate responses to praise • Student identifies common appropriate/inappropriate responses to praise in the classroom • Student names 5 common appropriate and 5 inappropriate responses to praise that people express	• Adult/peer discusses appropriate/inappropriate responses to praise • Student identifies common appropriate responses to praise in work settings and in the community • Student names 5 common appropriate and 5 inappropriate responses to praise expressed in work settings and in the community

PERSONAL-SOCIAL SKILLS

PERSONAL-SOCIAL SKILLS

	• Student develops list and teacher lists on chart or chalkboard several common appropriate/inappropriate responses to praise • Student develops poster by cutting and pasting common appropriate/inappropriate responses to praise listed in magazines and newspapers from the chart or chalkboard lists • Student seeks assistance from teacher	• Student identifies appropriate/inappropriate responses to praise found in work settings and in the community listed in magazines newspapers • Student seeks assistance from adult/peer
3. Respond to receiving praise	• Student role plays responding to receiving praise • Student appropriately receives praise in the classroom • Student seeks assistance from teacher	• Student asks supervisor in training program or job placement or an adult in the community to evaluate responses to receiving praise • Student appropriately receives praise in training programs or job placements and in the community • Student seeks assistance from adult/peer
4. Identify critical statements	• Counselor discusses with students critical statements made by people • Student identifies common critical statements people express • Student names 5 common critical statements expressed in work settings and in the community • Student develops list and teacher lists on chart or chalkboard several common critical statements expressed daily • Student develops poster by cutting and pasting pictures from magazines of people making common critical statements listed on chart or chalkboard • Student seeks assistance from teacher	• Adult/peer discusses with student critical statements made by people • Student identifies common critical statements expressed in work settings and in the community • Student names 5 common critical personal behaviors that people exhibit in work settings and in the community • Student identifies critical work statements listed in magazines, "world of work" textbooks, and newspapers • Student seeks assistance from adult/peer
5. Identify appropriate/ inappropriate responses to criticism	• Counselor discusses appropriate/inappropriate responses to criticism • Student role plays common appropriate/inappropriate responses to criticism in the classroom • Student names 5 common appropriate and 5 inappropriate responses to criticism that people express • Student develops list and teacher lists on chart or chalkboard several common appropriate/inappropriate responses to criticism • Student develops poster by cutting and pasting common appropriate/inappropriate responses to criticism listed in magazines and newspapers from the chart or chalkboard lists • Student seeks assistance from teacher	• Adult/peer discusses appropriate/inappropriate responses to criticism • Student role plays common appropriate/inappropriate responses to criticism in work settings and the community • Student names 5 common appropriate and 5 inappropriate responses to criticism expressed in work settings and in the community • Student identifies appropriate/inappropriate responses to criticism found in work settings and in the community listed in magazines and newspapers • Student seeks assistance from adult/peer
6. Respond to accepting criticism	• Student role plays responding to accepting criticism • Student appropriately accepts criticism in the classroom	• Student asks supervisor in training program or job placement or an adult in the community to evaluate responses to accepting criticism

• Student seeks assistance from teacher	• Student appropriately accepts criticism in training programs or job placements and in the community • Student seeks assistance from adult/peer

Domain: Personal-Social Skills
Competency 10: Exhibiting Socially Responsible Behavior
Subcompetency 37: Demonstrate Appropriate Behavior

Objectives	Training Activities	Home-/Community-Based Training Activities
1. Identify appropriate/ inappropriate behavior at home	• Counselor discusses appropriate/inappropriate behavior at home • Student identifies 5 appropriate and 5 inappropriate behaviors exhibited in the home • Student names 5 appropriate and 5 inappropriate behaviors exhibited in the home and the teacher lists them on chart/chalkboard • Student seeks assistance from teacher	• Adult/peer discusses appropriate/inappropriate behavior at home • Student describes 5 appropriate and 5 inappropriate behaviors exhibited in the workplace to an adult/peer • Student names 5 appropriate and 5 inappropriate behaviors exhibited in the workplace and adult/peer lists them on chart or notepad • Student seeks assistance from adult/peer
2. Identify appropriate/ inappropriate behavior at work	• Counselor discusses appropriate/inappropriate behavior at work • Student identifies 5 appropriate and 5 inappropriate behaviors exhibited at work • Student names 5 appropriate and 5 inappropriate behaviors exhibited at work and the teacher lists them on chart or chalkboard • Student seeks assistance from teacher	• Adult/peer discusses appropriate/inappropriate behavior at work • Student describes 5 appropriate and 5 inappropriate behaviors exhibited at work to a supervisor • Student names 5 appropriate and 5 inappropriate behaviors exhibited at work and a supervisor lists them on chart/notepad • Student seeks assistance from adult/peer
3. Identify appropriate/ inappropriate behavior at training programs	• Counselor discusses appropriate/inappropriate behavior at training programs • Student identifies 5 appropriate and 5 inappropriate behaviors exhibited at a training program • Student names 5 appropriate and 5 inappropriate behaviors exhibited at a training program and the teacher lists them on chart or chalkboard • Student seeks assistance from teacher	• Adult/peer discusses appropriate/inappropriate behavior at training programs • Student describes 5 appropriate and 5 inappropriate behaviors exhibited at a training program to a supervisor • Student names 5 appropriate and 5 inappropriate behaviors exhibited at a training program and a supervisor lists them on chart or notepad • Student seeks assistance from adult/peer
4. Identify appropriate/ inappropriate behavior in the community	• Counselor discusses appropriate/inappropriate behavior in the community • Student identifies 5 appropriate and 5 inappropriate behaviors exhibited in the community • Student names 5 appropriate and 5 inappropriate behaviors exhibited at work and the teacher lists them on chart or chalkboard • Student seeks assistance from teacher	• Adult/peer discusses appropriate/inappropriate behavior in the community • Student describes 5 appropriate and 5 inappropriate behaviors exhibited in the community to an adult/peer • Student names 5 appropriate and 5 inappropriate behaviors exhibited in the community and an adult/peer lists them on chart/notepad • Student seeks assistance from adult/peer
5. Practice appropriate behavior at home	• Student demonstrates appropriate behavior at home in role-play scenarios	• Student demonstrates appropriate ways to behave in the home with adults/peers

PERSONAL-SOCIAL SKILLS

	• Student demonstrates examples of appropriate behavior in the home and in the classroom • Student teams practice exhibiting appropriate behavior at home and monitor daily and report at end of each day • Student seeks assistance from teacher	• Student seeks assistance from adult/peer
6. Practice appropriate behavior at work	• Student demonstrates appropriate behavior at work in role play scenarios • Student demonstrates examples of appropriate behavior at work in the classroom • Student teams practice exhibiting appropriate behavior at work and monitor daily and report at end of each day • Student seeks assistance from teacher	• Student demonstrates appropriate ways to behave at work with adults/peers • Student seeks assistance from adult/peer
7. Practice appropriate behavior at school/training program	• Student demonstrates appropriate behavior at school/training program in role-play scenarios • Student demonstrates examples of appropriate behavior at school/training program in the classroom • Student teams practice exhibiting appropriate behavior at school/training program and monitor daily and report at end of each day • Student seeks assistance from teacher	• Student demonstrates appropriate ways to behave at school/training program with adults/peers • Student seeks assistance from adult/peer
8. Practice appropriate behavior in the community	• Student demonstrates appropriate behavior in the community in role-play scenarios • Student demonstrates examples of appropriate behavior at work and in the classroom • Student teams practice exhibiting appropriate behavior in the community and monitor daily and report at end of each day • Student seeks assistance from teacher	• Student demonstrates appropriate ways to behave in the community with adults/peers • Student seeks assistance from adult/peer

Domain: Personal-Social Skills
Competency 10: Exhibiting Socially Responsible Behavior
Subcompetency 38: Identify Current and Future Personal Roles

Objectives	Training Activities	Home-/Community-Based Training Activities
1. Identify current personal roles	• Teacher describes her/his current personal roles and examples of other people's personal roles • Student names possible current personal roles • Student develops list and teacher lists on chart or chalkboard several possible current personal roles	• Adult/peer describes student's current personal roles and examples of other people's personal roles • Student demonstrates an understanding of current personal work roles • Student identifies possible current work role from pictures in magazines or "world of work" textbooks and newspapers

Objectives	Training Activities	Home-/Community-Based Training Activities
	• Student develops poster by cutting and pasting pictures from magazines of people demonstrating possible current personal roles listed on chart or chalkboard • Student seeks assistance from teacher	• Student seeks assistance from adult/peer
2. Identify possible future personal roles	• Teacher describes student's possible future personal roles • Student names possible future personal roles • Student develops list and teacher lists on chart or chalkboard several possible future personal roles • Student develops poster by cutting and pasting pictures from magazines of people demonstrating possible future personal roles listed on chart or chalkboard • Student seeks assistance from teacher	• Adult/peer describes student's possible future personal roles • Student demonstrates an understanding of future personal work roles • Student identifies possible future work roles from pictures in magazines or "world of work" textbooks and newspapers • Student seeks assistance from adult/peer
3. Describe how personal roles differ from those of significant others	• Student discusses the differences between her/his current and/or future personal roles and those of her/his significant others • Student lists on chart/chalkboard her/his own current and/or future personal roles and her/his significant others' current and future personal roles	• Student discusses the differences between her/his personal current and/or future work roles and those of her/his significant others • Student lists with adults/peers her/his own personal current and/or future work roles and her/his significant others' personal current and future work roles
4. Describe how personal roles interact with others' roles	• Student discusses how her/his current and/or future personal roles interact with that of her/his significant others • Student lists on chart/chalkboard her/his own current and/or future personal roles and how they interact with her/his significant others' current and future personal roles • Student seeks assistance from teacher	• Student discusses how her/his own personal current and/or future work roles interact with those of her/his significant others • Student lists with adults/peers how her/his own personal current and/or future work roles interact with those of her/his significant others on notepad/chart • Student seeks assistance from adult/peer

PERSONAL-SOCIAL SKILLS

Domain: Personal-Social Skills
Competency 10: Exhibiting Socially Responsible Behavior
Subcompetency 39: Demonstrate Respect for Others' Rights and Property

Objectives	Training Activities	Home-/Community-Based Training Activities
1. Identify personal property and rights of others	• Teacher describes student's personal property and rights of others and examples of others' personal property • Student lists on chart/chalkboard her/his own personal property and the rights of others to her/his personal property • Student lists on chart/chalkboard others' personal property and her/his rights to others' personal property • Student seeks assistance from teacher	• Adult/peer describes student's personal property and rights of others and examples of others' personal property • Student lists with supervisor her/his personal property that should accompany her/him at training programs or job placements and the rights of others to her/his personal property on notepad/chart • Student lists with supervisor others' personal property that could accompany them at training programs or job placements and others' rights to her/his personal property on notepad/chart

PERSONAL-SOCIAL SKILLS

		• Student lists with adult/peer her/his personal property in the community and the rights of others to her/his personal property on notepad/chart • Student lists with adult/peer others' personal property in the community and others' rights to her/his personal property on note-pad/chart • Student seeks assistance from adult/peer
2. Identify reasons for respecting personal property and rights of others	• Teacher describes reasons for respecting personal property and rights of others • Student lists on chart/chalkboard reasons for respecting others' personal property and rights of others on notepad/chart • Student role plays scenarios depicting the reasons for respecting the personal property and rights of others	• Adult/peer describes reasons for respecting personal property and rights of others • Student lists with supervisor the reasons for respecting others' personal property rights at training programs or job placements • Student lists with adult/peer the reasons for respecting others' personal property and rights in the community
3. Practice respecting others' personal property and rights	• Student self-monitors daily on a classroom chart his/her practice of respecting other class members' personal property and rights • Student role plays scenarios depicting the practice of respecting other class members, personal property and rights • Student teams practice respecting team members' personal property and rights and monitor daily and report at end of each day • Student seeks assistance from teacher	• Student is evaluated by supervisor at training program or job placements on his/her practice of respecting others' personal property and rights • Student is evaluated by adult/peer on his/her practice of respecting others' personal property and rights in the community • Student seeks assistance from adult/peer
4. Identify actions for borrowing items	• Teacher describes and demonstrates actions for borrowing items • Student lists on chalkboard/chart the appropriate actions for borrowing items • Student role plays scenarios depicting the appropriate actions for borrowing items • Student seeks assistance from teacher	• Adult/peer describes and demonstrates actions for borrowing items • Student lists with supervisor on notepad/chart the appropriate actions for borrowing items at training programs or job placements • Student lists with adult/peer on notepad/chart the appropriate actions for borrowing items in the community • Student seeks assistance from adult/peer
5. Identify actions when others' personal property has been damaged	• Teacher describes and demonstrates appropriate actions when others' personal property has been damaged • Guest speaker discusses the appropriate actions that should be taken when others' personal property has been damaged • Student lists on chalkboard/chart the appropriate actions that should be taken when others' personal property has been damaged • Student role plays scenarios depicting the appropriate actions for when others' personal property has been damaged • Student seeks assistance from teacher	• Adult/peer describes and demonstrates appropriate actions when others' personal property has been damaged • Supervisor discusses the appropriate actions that should be taken when others' personal property in training programs or job placements has been damaged • Adult/peer discusses the appropriate actions that should be taken when others' personal property in the community has been damaged • Student lists with supervisor on notepad/chart the appropriate actions that should be taken when others' personal property in training programs or job placements has been damaged

		• Student lists with adult/peer the appropriate actions that should be taken when others' personal property in the community has been damaged • Student seeks assistance from adult/peer
6. Identify actions when others' personal rights have been violated	• Guest speaker discusses the appropriate actions that should be taken when others' personal rights have been violated • Student lists on chalkboard/chart the appropriate actions that should be taken when others' personal rights have been violated • Student role plays scenarios depicting the appropriate actions that should be taken when others' personal rights have been violated • Student seeks assistance from teacher	• Supervisor discusses the appropriate actions that should be taken when others' personal rights in training programs or job placements have been violated • Adult/peer discusses the appropriate actions that should be taken when others' personal rights in the community have been violated • Student lists with supervisor on notepad/chart the appropriate actions that should be taken when others' personal rights in training programs or job placements have been violated • Student lists with adult/peer the appropriate actions that should be taken when others' personal rights in the community have been violated • Student seeks assistance from adult/peer

Domain: Personal-Social Skills
Competency 10: Exhibiting Socially Responsible Behavior
Subcompetency 40: Demonstrate Respect for Authority

Objectives	Training Activities	Home-/Community-Based Training Activities
1. Identify authority figures	• Teacher identifies authority figures at school • Student lists on chalkboard/chart individuals who are to be respected as authority • Teacher discusses who are authority individuals at school • Speaker discusses figures who are typically regarded as being authorities • Student seeks assistance from teacher	• Adult/peer identifies authority figures in community • Supervisor discusses authority figures in training programs or job placements • Adult/peer discusses authority figures in the community • Supervisor and student list on notepad/chart 5 individuals who are authority figures at training programs or job placements • Student seeks assistance from adult/peer
2. Identify roles of authority figures	• Teacher discusses the roles of authority figures and how and why we respect these individuals • Guest speaker identifies the roles of those individuals in position of authority and how and why we show them respect • Student lists on chalkboard/chart 5 different roles of authority figures	• Supervisor discusses the roles of authority figures in training programs or job placements and how and why we show them respect • Adult/peer identifies the roles of authority figures in the community and how and why we show them respect • Supervisor and student list on notepad/chart 5 different roles of authority figures • Adult/peer lists on notepad/chart 5 different roles of authority figures in the community
3. Identify consequences of not respecting authority	• Guest speaker discusses the consequences of not respecting authority in school or in the community	• Supervisor discusses with student the consequences of not respecting authority in training programs or job placements

PERSONAL-SOCIAL SKILLS

PERSONAL-SOCIAL SKILLS

	• Teacher identifies the consequences of not respecting authority • Student lists on chalkboard/chart 5 consequences of not respecting authority	• Adult/peer identifies the consequences of not respecting authority in the community • Supervisor and student list on notepad/chart 5 consequences of not respecting authority in training programs or job placements • Adult/peer lists on notepad/chart 5 consequences of not respecting authority in the community
4. Practice respecting authority	• Student self-monitors daily on a classroom chart her/his practice of respecting authority figures in school • Student role plays scenarios depicting the practice of respecting authority in school • Student teams practice respecting authority and monitor daily and report at end of each day • Student seeks assistance from teacher	• Student is evaluated by supervisor at training program or job placements on her/his practice of respecting authority figures • Student is evaluated by adult/peer on her/his practice of respecting authority figures in the community • Student seeks assistance from adult/peer

Domain: Personal-Social Skills
Competency 10: Exhibiting Socially Responsible Behavior
Subcompetency 41: Demonstrate Ability to Follow Directions/Instructions

Objectives	*Training Activities*	*Home-/Community-Based Training Activities*
1. Identify importance of following authority directions/instructions	• Teacher discusses importance of following authority directions/instructions • Student lists on chalkboard/chart the importance of following authority directions in school • Teacher discusses the importance of following authority directions/instructions in school • Guest speaker discusses the importance of following authority directions/instructions in school or in the community	• Adult/peer discusses the importance of following authority directions/instructions in the community • Supervisor discusses the importance of following authority directions/instructions in training programs or job placements
2. Identify actions of not following authority directions/instructions	• Teacher discusses actions of not following authority directions/instructions • Guest speaker discusses the consequences of not following authority directions/instructions in school or in the community • Teacher discusses the consequences of not following authority directions/instructions in school • Student lists on chalkboard/chart 5 consequences of not following authority directions/instructions	• Adult/peer discusses actions of not following authority directions/instructions in the community • Supervisor discusses with student the consequences of not following authority directions/instructions in training program or job placements • Adult/peer discusses the consequences of not following authority directions/instructions in the community • Supervisor and student lists on notepad/chart 5 consequences of not following authority directions/instructions in training programs or job placements • Adult/peer lists on notepad/chart 5 consequences of not following authority directions/instructions in the community

3. Practice following authority directions/instructions	• Student self-monitors daily on a classroom chart his/her practice of following authority directions/instructions in school • Student role plays scenarios depicting the practice of following authority directions/instructions in school • Student teams practice following directions/instructions and monitor daily and report at end of each day	• Student is evaluated by supervisor at training program or job placements on his/her practice of following authority directions/instructions • Student is evaluated by adult/peer on his/her practice of following authority directions/instructions in the community

Domain: Personal-Social Skills
Competency 10: Exhibiting Socially Responsible Behavior
Subcompetency 42: Demonstrate Appropriate Citizen Rights and Responsibilities

Objectives	Training Activities	Home-/Community-Based Training Activities
1. Identify community services available to citizens	• Teacher discusses available community services • Student develops a collage depicting available community services • Student lists on chalkboard/chart available community services	• Adult/peer discusses available community services • Supervisor discusses with student available community employment services • Adult/peer lists on notepad/chart 5 available community services
2. Locate community services available to citizens	• Teacher discusses available community services locations • Student uses a telephone directory and local map and student and teacher locate available utility services • Student uses a telephone directory and local map and student and teacher locate available medical services • Student uses a telephone directory and local map and student and teacher locate available transportation services • Student uses a telephone directory and local map and student and teacher locate available government services • Student uses a telephone directory and local map and student and teacher locate available miscellaneous services • Student seeks assistance from teacher	• Adult/peer discusses available community services locations • Supervisor and student locate available community employment services • Student seeks assistance from adult/peer
3. Identify major rights of citizens	• Teacher discusses the major rights of citizens • Guest speaker discusses the major rights of citizens in the United States • Student lists on chalkboard/chart 5 different rights of citizens • Student develops poster depicting the rights of citizens • Student seeks assistance from teacher	• Supervisor discusses the major rights of students in training programs or job placements • Adult/peer discusses the major rights of citizens in the community • Supervisor and student list on notepad/chart 5 different rights students have in training programs or job placements • Adult/peer lists on notepad/chart 5 different rights of citizens in the community • Student seeks assistance from adult/peer

PERSONAL-SOCIAL SKILLS

PERSONAL-SOCIAL SKILLS

4. Identify major responsibilities of citizens	• Teacher discusses the major responsibilities of citizens • Guest speaker discusses the major responsibilities of citizens in the United States • Student lists on chalkboard/chart 5 different responsibilities of citizens • Student develops poster depicting the responsibilities of citizens • Student seeks assistance from teacher	• Supervisor discusses the major responsibilities of students in training programs or job placements • Adult/peer discusses the major responsibilities of citizens in the community • Supervisor and student list on notepad/chart 5 different responsibilities students have in training programs or job placements • Adult/peer lists on notepad/chart 5 different responsibilities of citizens in the community • Student seeks assistance from adult/peer
5. Identify citizens' duties to governments	• Teacher discusses the major duties of citizens • Guest speaker discusses the major rights of citizens in the United States • Student lists on chalkboard/chart 5 different duties citizens have to the government • Student develops poster depicting citizens' duties to governments • Student seeks assistance from teacher	• Adult/peer discusses the major duties citizens have in the community • Adult/peer lists 5 major duties citizens have in the community • Student seeks assistance from adult/peer
6. Practice being a good citizen	• Student self-monitors daily on a classroom chart her/his practice of being a good citizen • Student role plays scenarios depicting the practice of being a good citizen • Student teams practice exhibiting good citizenship and monitor daily and report at end of each day	• Student is evaluated by supervisor at training program or job placements on her/his practice of being a good citizen • Student is evaluated by adult/peer on her/his practice of being a good citizen

Domain: Personal-Social Skills
Competency 10: Exhibiting Socially Responsible Behavior
Subcompetency 43: Identify How Personal Behavior Affects Others

Objectives	Training Activities	Home-/Community-Based Training Activities
1. Identify how personal behavior can affect others	• Guest speaker discusses how appropriate and inappropriate personal behaviors affect others positively or negatively • Teacher discusses how appropriate or inappropriate personal behaviors affect others in school positively or negatively • Student lists on chalkboard/chart 5 appropriate and 5 inappropriate personal behaviors and how they affect others in school positively or negatively • Student seeks assistance from teacher	• Supervisor discusses with student how appropriate and inappropriate personal behaviors affect other students in training programs or job placements positively or negatively • Adult/peer discusses how appropriate or inappropriate personal behaviors affect others in the community positively or negatively • Supervisor and student list on notepad/chart 5 appropriate and 5 inappropriate personal behaviors and how they affect other students in training programs and job placements positively or negatively • Adult/peer lists on notepad/chart 5 appropriate and 5 inappropriate personal behaviors and how they affect others in the community positively or negatively • Student seeks assistance from adult/peer

2. Identify cues others provide when personal behavior is inappropriate	• Guest speaker discusses cues others give to let you know when your personal behavior is inappropriate in school • Teacher discusses cues others give to let you know when your personal behavior affects others in school • Student lists on chalkboard/chart 5 cues others give to let you know when personal behavior in school is inappropriate • Student seeks assistance from teacher	• Supervisor discusses with student cues others provide at training programs or job placements when personal behavior is inappropriate • Adult/peer discusses cues others give to let you know when your personal behavior is inappropriate in the community • Supervisor and student list on notepad/chart 5 cues others give to let you know when personal behavior in training programs or job placements is inappropriate • Adult/peer lists on notepad/chart 5 cues others give to let you know when personal behavior is inappropriate in the community • Student seeks assistance from adult/peer
3. Describe ways to change inappropriate behavior	• Teacher discusses the importance of knowing how to change inappropriate personal behaviors and describes strategies for changing behavior in school • Student lists on chalkboard/chart ways that he/she can change inappropriate personal behavior in school • Guest speaker discusses the importance of knowing how to change inappropriate personal behaviors and describes strategies for changing behavior • Student seeks assistance from teacher	• Adult/peer discusses the importance of knowing how to change inappropriate personal behavior exhibited in the community • Supervisor discusses the importance of knowing how to change inappropriate personal behaviors exhibited in training programs or at job placements • Student seeks assistance from adult/peer

Domain: Personal-Social Skills
Competency 11: Developing and Maintaining Appropriate Social Relationships
Subcompetency 44: Develop Friendships

Objectives	Training Activities	Home-/Community-Based Training Activities
1. Identify why friendship is important	• Teacher discusses the reasons for having friends in school • Student lists on chalkboard/chart why it is important to have friends at school • Speaker discusses the importance of having friends at school or in the community	• Adult/peer discusses the importance of having friends in the community • Supervisor discusses the importance of having friends at training programs or job placements • Student names 2 reasons why it is important for having friends in the community, at training programs, or at job placements
2. Identify characteristics of friendship	• Teacher discusses the characteristics of school friendships • Student lists on chalkboard/chart the characteristics of school friendships • Speaker discusses the characteristics involved in school and/or community friendships	• Adult/peer discusses the characteristics of community friendships • Supervisor discusses the characteristics of training program or job friendships • Student names 5 characteristics of friendships in the community, at training programs, or job placements
3. Describe how to select a friend	• Teacher describes how to select friends at school	• Adult/peer describes how to select friends in the community

PERSONAL-SOCIAL SKILLS

	• Student lists on chalkboard/chart the process of selecting friends at school • Guest speaker discusses the process of selecting friends at school and in the community	• Supervisor describes how to select friends in training programs or job placements
4. Practice developing friends	• Student self-monitors daily on a classroom chart her/his practice of developing friends at school • Student role plays scenarios depicting the practice of developing friendships • Student teams practice developing friends and monitor daily and report at end of each day • Student seeks assistance from teacher	• Student is evaluated by supervisor at training program or job placement on her/his practice of developing friendships • Student is evaluated by adult/peer on her/his practice of developing friendships • Student seeks assistance from adult/peer

Domain: Personal-Social Skills
Competency 11: Developing and Maintaining Appropriate Social Relationships
Subcompetency 45: Maintain Friendships

Objectives	Training Activities	Home-/Community-Based Training Activities
1. Identify ways to keep and lose friends	• Teacher discusses ways to keep and lose friends in school • Student lists on chalkboard/chart ways to keep and lose friends at school • Guest speaker discusses ways to keep and lose friends at school or in the community • Student seeks assistance from teacher	• Adult/peer discusses the ways to keep and lose friends in the community • Supervisor discusses the ways to keep and lose friends at training programs or job placements • Student names 5 ways to keep friends and 5 ways to lose friends in the community, at training programs, or at job placements • Student seeks assistance from adult/peer
2. Identify how to select a date	• Teacher demonstrates how to select a date at school • Student lists on chalkboard/chart ways to select a date at school • Speaker demonstrates ways to select a date at school or in the community • Student seeks assistance from teacher	• Adult/peer demonstrates how to select a date in the community • Supervisor demonstrates the ways to select a date at training programs or job placements • Student names 5 ways to select a date in the community, at training programs, or at job placements • Student seeks assistance from adult/peer
3. Identify procedures for dating	• Teacher discusses the activities of dating • Student lists on chalkboard/chart some of the activities of dating • Counselor discusses appropriate dating activities in the community • Student role plays dating scenarios • Student seeks assistance from teacher	• Adult/peer discusses the activities of dating in the community • Supervisor discusses the activities of dating in the community • Student names appropriate activities related to dating in the community • Student practices dating with chaperone • Student seeks assistance from adult/peer
4. Identify appropriate responses to intimacy with close friends	• Teacher discusses appropriate acts of intimacy with close friends	• Adult/peer discusses appropriate acts of intimacy in the community with close friends

PERSONAL-SOCIAL SKILLS

• Student lists on chalkboard/chart appropriate acts of intimacy and privacy concerns • Counselor discusses appropriate imtimacy activities in the community and privacy concerns with close friends • Student role plays appropriate public acts of intimacy with close friends • Student seeks assistance from teacher	• Supervisor discusses the acts of intimacy in in the community that are appropriate and inappropriate and privacy concerns • Student names appropriate and inappropriate acts of intimacy and the appropriate locations with close friends • Student practices exhibiting appropriate acts of intimacy in the community with close friends • Student seeks assistance from adult/peer

5. Practice maintaining friendships

• Student role plays acts for maintaining friendships in the classroom • Student keeps journal/checklist of personal friendships and shares with teacher for feedback and assistance • Student teams work on maintaining friendship and report daily on the their success • Student seeks assistance from teacher	• Supervisor assists student in maintaining friendships • Student keeps journal/checklist of personal friendships and shares with adult/peer for feedback and assistance • Student seeks assistance from adult/peer

Domain: Personal-Social Skills
Competency 12: Exhibiting Independent Behavior
Subcompetency 46: Set and Reach Personal Goals

Objectives	*Training Activities*	*Home-/Community-Based Training Activities*
1. Identify the importance of setting personal goals	• Teacher discusses the reasons for setting and reaching personal goals in school and in the community • Student lists on chalkboard/chart why it is important to set and reach personal school and community goals • Guest speaker discusses the importance of setting and reaching school and community personal goals • Student seeks assistance from teacher	• Adult/peer discusses the importance of setting and reaching personal community-related goals • Supervisor discusses the importance of setting and reaching training program or job placement goals • Student names 2 reasons why it is important to set and reach personal community training program or job placement goals • Student seeks assistance from adult/peer
2. Identify how to set goals	• Teacher describes how to set school and community goals • Student lists on chalkboard/chart ways to set school and community goals • Counselor identifies ways to set school or community goals • Student seeks assistance from teacher	• Adult/peer describes how to set community-related goals • Supervisor discusses the ways to set training program or job placement goals • Student names 5 ways to set community, training program, or job placement goals • Student seeks assistance from adult/peer
3. Identify reasons to reach goals	• Teacher discusses reasons to reach school and community goals • Student lists on chart/chalkboard reasons for reaching personal goals at school or in the community • Student role plays scenarios depicting the reasons for reaching personal goals at school or in the community • Student seeks assistance from teacher	• Adult/peer discusses reasons to reach community-related goals • Student lists with supervisor the reasons for reaching personal training program or job placement goals • Student lists with adult/peer the reasons for reaching personal community goals • Student seeks assistance from adult/peer

4. Identify how to modify/revise goals	• Teacher describes how to modify/revise personal school and community goals • Student lists on chalkboard/chart ways to modify/revise personal goals at school and in the community • Counselor describes ways to modify/revise school or community goals • Student seeks assistance from teacher	• Adult/peer describes how to modify/revise personal community-related goals • Supervisor describes the ways to modify/revise training program or job placement goals • Student names 5 ways to modify/revise a community goal • Student seeks assistance from adult/peer
5. Practice setting and meeting goals	• Student self-monitors daily on a classroom chart his/her practice of setting and meeting goals • Student role plays scenarios depicting the practice of setting and meeting goals • Student teams set individual goals and monitor each other's goals on a daily basis and report at end of each day whether or not they met set goals • Student seeks assistance from teacher	• Student is evaluated by supervisor at training program or job placement on his/her practice of setting and meeting goals • Student is evaluated by adult/peer on his/her practice of setting and meeting goals in the community • Student seeks assistance from adult/peer

Domain: Personal-Social Skills
Competency 12: Exhibiting Independent Behavior
Subcompetency 47: Demonstrate Self-Organization

Objectives	*Training Activities*	*Home-/Community-Based Training Activities*
1. Identify routine daily activities	• Teacher demonstrates routine daily activities at home and in school • Student lists on chalkboard/chart some of the routine daily activities that take place in school and at home • Counselor discusses appropriate routine daily activities that are conducted at school and in the home • Student role plays conducting daily routines that occur in the school and in the home • Student seeks assistance from teacher	• Adult/peer demonstrates routine daily activities in the community and in job placements • Supervisor demonstrates some of the daily routine activities that take place in the community and in job placements • Student names appropriate activities that are conducted daily in the community and in job placements • Student practices conducting daily routines that occur in the community and in job placements • Student seeks assistance from adult/peer
2. Develop plan of daily activities	• Student devises a plan outlining personal daily activities in school and at home • Student plans approximate time of day for daily routine activities in school and in the home • Student develops poster/calendar depicting normal/routine daily activities at school and in the home using pictures and/or descriptions • Student seeks assistance from teacher	• Student writes out a plan outlining personal daily activities in the community and in job placements • Student lists approximate time for conducting routine daily activities in the community and in job placements • Student seeks assistance from adult/peer
3. Identify areas of responsibility in personal life	• Teacher discusses the major responsibilities of a citizen's personal life at school and at home • Principal discusses the major responsibilities of a citizen's personal life in school and in the home	• Supervisor discusses the major responsibilities of the student in her/his personal life in the community or in job placements • Adult/peer discusses the major responsibilities of a citizen's personal life in the community

PERSONAL-SOCIAL SKILLS

Objectives	Training Activities	Home-/Community-Based Training Activities
	• Student lists on chalkboard/chart 5 different responsibilities of citizens' personal life • Student develops poster depicting the responsibilities of a citizen's personal life at school or in the home • Student seeks assistance from teacher	• Supervisor and student list on notepad/chart 5 different personal life responsibilities the student has in training programs or job placements • Adult/peer lists on notepad/chart 5 different responsibilities of a citizen's personal life in the community • Student seeks assistance from adult/peer
4. Identify importance of organizing personal activities	• Teacher discusses the importance of organizing personal activities • Student lists on chalkboard/chart the importance of being organized in school and at home • Teacher discusses the importance of being organized at school and at home • Guest speaker discusses the importance of being organized in school, at home, or in the community • Student seeks assistance from teacher	• Adult/peer discusses the importance of organizing personal activities • Supervisor discusses the importance of being organized at training programs or at job placements • Adult/peer discusses the importance of being organized in the community • Student seeks assistance from adult/peer
5. Practice daily self-organization	• Student identifies daily self-organization strategies and practices at school and in her/his home • Student develops self-monitoring plan for being organized daily in school and in her/his home • Student demonstrates daily self-organization at school and in her/his home • Student seeks assistance from teacher	• Student describes daily self-organization strategies and practices in job placements and in the community • Student develops self-monitoring plan for being organized daily in job placements and in the community • Student demonstrates self-organization daily in job placements and in the community • Student seeks assistance from adult/peer
6. Request assistance with self-organization	• Teacher identifies sources for assisting student with self-organization • Student identifies sources of assistance to help with self-organization • Student role plays seeking assistance with self-organization in school or at home • Student requests assistance with self-organization	• Adult/peer identifies sources for assisting student with self-organization • Student demonstrates how to request assistance in being self-organized in job placements and in the community • Student requests assistance with self-organization in the community or in job placements

Domain: Personal-Social Skills
Competency 12: Exhibiting Independent Behavior
Subcompetency 48: Demonstrate Self-Determination

Objectives	Training Activities	Home-/Community-Based Training Activities
1. Identify importance of practicing self-determination	• Teacher discusses the importance of practicing self-determination • Student lists on chalkboard/chart the importance of exhibiting self-determination in school and at home • Teacher discusses the importance of exhibiting self-determination at school and at home	• Adult/peer discusses the importance of practicing self-determination • Supervisor discusses the importance of exhibiting self-determination at training programs or at job placements • Adult/peer discusses the importance of exhibiting self-determination in the community

PERSONAL-SOCIAL SKILLS

PERSONAL-SOCIAL SKILLS

	• Guest speaker discusses the importance of exhibiting self-determination in school, at home, and in the community	
2. Practice self-determination	• Student identifies daily self-determination strategies and practices at school and in her/his home • Student develops self-monitoring plan for using self-determination skills daily in school and in her/his home • Student demonstrates daily self-determination skills at school and in the community	• Student identifies daily self-determination strategies and practices in job placements and in the community • Student develops self-monitoring plan for using self-determination skills daily in job placements and in the community • Student demonstrates self-determination skills at job placements and in the community
3. Request assistance with self-determination	• Student identifies sources of assistance with using self-determination skills in her/his school and at home • Student role plays seeking assistance to use self-determination skills in her/his school or at home • Student requests assistance to use self-determination skills	• Student demonstrates how to request assistance to use self-determination skills in job placements and in the community • Student requests assistance to use self-determination skills in the community or in job placements

Domain: Personal-Social Skills
Competency 13: Making Informed Decisions
Subcompetency 49: Identify Problems/Conflicts

Objectives	Training Activities	Home-/Community-Based Training Activities
1. Identify personal problems/conflicts	• Teacher discusses possible personal problems/conflicts that can occur in school or at home • Student lists on chalkboard/chart personal problems/conflicts that can occur in school and at home • Teacher discusses some of the personal problems/conflicts that can occur in school and at home • Student seeks assistance from teacher	• Adult/peer discusses possible personal problems/conflicts that can occur in the community • Supervisor discusses personal problems/conflicts that can occur at training programs or at job placements • Adult/peer discusses personal problems/conflicts that can occur in the community • Student seeks assistance from adult/peer
2. Identify why personal problems/conflicts exist	• Teacher discusses some of the reasons why personal problems/conflicts arise in school or at home • Student lists on chalkboard/chart some of the reasons why personal problems arise in school or at home • Guest speaker discusses some of the major reasons why personal problems/conflicts arise in school, at home, or in the community • Student seeks assistance from teacher	• Supervisor discusses some of the reasons why personal problems/conflicts arise in work training programs or job placements • Adult/peer discusses some of the reasons why personal problems/conflicts arise in the community • Student names 2 reasons why personal problems arise for each: work training programs, job placements, or in the community • Student seeks assistance from adult/peer

3. Request assistance in identify-ing personal problems/conflicts	• Student identifies sources of assistance for helping him/her resolve personal problems/conflicts at school or in the home • Student role plays seeking assistance with resolving personal problems/conflicts in school or at home • Student requests assistance with resolving personal problems/conflicts at school or in the home	• Student demonstrates how to request assistance in resolving personal problems/conflicts in job placements and in the community • Student requests assistance with resolving personal problems/conflicts in job place-ments and in the community

Domain: Personal-Social Skills
Competency 13: Making Informed Decisions
Subcompetency 50: Use Appropriate Resources to Assist in Problem Solving

Objectives	Training Activities	Home-/Community-Based Training Activities
1. Identify situations in which individuals need advice	• Teacher identifies possible situations requiring advice • Student lists on chalkboard/chart situations in which individuals need assistance or advice in school and at home • Teacher identifies some of the more com-mon situations in which individuals need assistance or advice at school and at home • Guest speaker discusses some of the situa-tions that arise in which individuals need assistance or advice at school, at home, or in the community • Student seeks assistance from teacher	• Adult/peer identifies possible situations requiring advice • Supervisor identifies situations in which individuals need assistance or advice at training programs or at job placements • Adult/peer identifies situations in which individuals need assistance or advice in the community • Student seeks assistance from adult/peer
2. Identify available sources for providing assistance in resolving personal problems/conflicts	• Teacher identifies available sources for providing assistance in resolving personal problems/conflicts • Student lists on chalkboard/chart sources for providing assistance in resolving per-sonal problems/conflicts in school and at home • Teacher discusses some of the more com-mon sources of support for providing assistance for resolving personal problems/conflicts in school and at home • Guest speaker discusses some of the more common sources of support for assisting in resolving personal problems/conflicts inschool, at home, or in the community	• Adult/peer identifies available sources for providing assistance in resolving personal problems/conflicts • Supervisor discusses sources for providing assistance in resolving personal problems/conflicts in training programs or at job placements • Adult/peer discusses sources for providing assistance in resolving personal problems/conflicts in the community
3. Identify outcomes of seeking help in resolving personal problems/conflicts	• Teacher identifies outcomes of seeking help in resolving personal problems/conflicts • Student lists on chalkboard/chart possible outcomes of resolving personal problems/conflicts in school or at home with help from sources of support	• Adult/peer identifies outcomes of seeking help in resolving personal problems/conflicts • Supervisor discusses possible outcomes of resolving personal problems/conflicts in training programs or at job placements with help from sources of support

PERSONAL-SOCIAL SKILLS

PERSONAL-SOCIAL SKILLS

	• Teacher discusses some of the more common outcomes of resolving personal problems/conflicts with help from sources of support in school or at home • Guest speaker identifies some of the more possible outcomes of resolving personal problems/conflicts in school, at home, or in the community with help from sources of support	• Adult/peer discusses possible outcomes of resolving personal problems/conflicts in the community with help from sources of support
4. Seek appropriate sources in helping to resolve personal problems/conflicts	• Student identifies sources of assistance with resolving personal problems/conflicts at school or in the home • Student role plays seeking assistance with resolving personal problems/conflicts at school or at home • Student seeks assistance with resolving personal problems/conflicts at school or in the home	• Student demonstrates how to seek assistance with resolving personal problems/conflicts in job placements and in the community • Student seeks assistance with resolving personal problems/conflicts in job placements and in the community

Domain: Personal-Social Skills
Competency 13: Making Informed Decisions
Subcompetency 51: Develop and Select Best Solution to Problems/Conflicts

Objectives	*Training Activities*	*Home-/Community-Based Training Activities*
1. Identify solutions to personal problems/conflicts	• Teacher identifies solutions to personal problems/conflicts • Student lists on chalkboard/chart solutions to identified personal problems/conflicts that can occur in school and at home • Teacher discusses some of the personal problems/conflicts that can occur in school and at home • Guest speaker discusses some of the solutions to identified personal problems/conflicts that can occur in school or in the community • Student seeks assistance from teacher	• Adult/peer identifies solutions to personal problems/conflicts • Supervisor discusses solutions to identified personal problems/conflicts that can occur at training programs or at job placements • Adult/peer discusses solutions to identified personal problems/conflicts that can occur in the community • Student seeks assistance from adult/peer
2. Select best solutions developed to personal problems/conflicts	• Student lists on chalkboard/chart the best solutions to identified personal problems/conflicts that can occur in school and home • Teacher discusses some of the best solutions to identified problems/conflicts that can occur at school and at home • Guest speaker discusses some of the best solutions to identified personal problems/conflicts that can occur in school or in the community	• Supervisor discusses the best solutions to identified personal problems/conflicts that can occur at training programs or at job placements • Adult/peer discusses the best solutions to identified personal problems/conflicts that can occur in the community
3. Seek assistance in helping to develop and select best solutions to personal problems/conflicts	• Student identifies sources of assistance in developing and selecting the best solutions to resolving personal problems/conflicts at school or at home	• Student demonstrates an understanding of how to seek assistance with developing and selecting the best solutions to resolving personal problems/conflicts in job placements and in the community

	• Student role plays seeking assistance with developing and selecting the best solutions to resolving personal problems/conflicts at school or at home • Student seeks assistance to help with developing and selecting the best solutions to resolving personal problems/conflicts at school or in the home	• Student seeks assistance with developing and selecting the best solutions to personal problems/conflicts in job placements and in the community
4. Practice developing and selecting best solutions to personal problems/conflicts	• Student develops and selects best solutions to resolving personal problems/conflicts in school and at home • Student develops self-monitoring plan for developing and selecting the best solutions to personal problems/conflicts in school and at home • Student demonstrates using the skills of selecting and developing the best solutions to resolving personal problems/conflicts in school and at home • Student seeks assistance from teacher	• Student identifies strategies for developing and selecting the best solutions to personal problems/conflicts in job placements and in the community • Student develops self-monitoring plan for developing and selecting the best solutions to personal problems/conflicts in job placements and in the community • Student demonstrates using the skills of selecting and developing the best solutions to resolving personal problems/conflicts at job placements and in the community • Student seeks assistance from adult/peer

Domain: Personal-Social Skills
Competency 13: Making Informed Decisions
Subcompetency 52: Demonstrate Decision Making

Objectives	Training Activities	Home-/Community-Based Training Activities
1. Identify importance of making decisions	• Teacher discusses importance of making decisions at school and home • Student lists on chalkboard/chart the importance of making decisions in school and at home • Teacher discusses the importance of making decisions in school or at home • Speaker discusses the importance of making decisions in school or in the community • Student seeks assistance from teacher	• Adult/peer discusses importance of making decisions in the community • Supervisor discusses the importance of making decisions in training programs or job placements • Adult/peer discusses the importance of making decisions in the community • Student seeks assistance from adult/peer
2. Identify steps in making informed decisions	• Student devises a plan outlining the steps in making informed decisions in school and at home • Student develops poster/calendar depicting the steps in making informed decisions at school and in the home using pictures and/or descriptions • Student seeks assistance from teacher	• Student writes out a plan outlining the steps for making informed decisions in training programs and in job placements • Student writes out a plan outlining the steps for making informed decisions in the community • Student seeks assistance from adult/peer
3. Seek help in making decisions	• Teacher identifies sources for helping in decision making • Student identifies sources of assistance in making informed decisions at school or at home	• Adult/peer identifies sources for helping in decision making • Student demonstrates how to seek assistance with making informed decisions in job placements and in the community

	• Student role plays seeking assistance with making informed decisions at school or at home • Student seeks assistance with making informed decisions at school or at home	• Student seeks assistance with making informed decisions in job placements and in the community

Domain: Personal-Social Skills
Competency 14: Communicating with Others
Subcompetency 53: Demonstrate Listening and Responding Skills

Objectives	Training Activities	Home-/Community-Based Training Activities
1. Identify the importance of listening and responding	• Teacher discusses importance of listening and responding at school and at home • Student lists on chalkboard/chart the importance of listening and responding in school and at home • Teacher discusses the importance of listening and responding in school and at home • Guest speaker discusses the importance of listening and responding in school or in the community	• Adult/peer discusses importance of listening and responding in the community • Supervisor discusses the importance of listening and responding at training programs or job placements • Adult/peer discusses the importance of listening and responding in the community
2. Identify appropriate listening techniques	• Teacher identifies appropriate listening techniques at school and at home • Student lists on chalkboard/chart the appropriate techniques for listening at school and at home • Teacher demonstrates some of the most appropriate listening techniques to use at school and at home • Guest speaker demonstrates some of the most appropriate listening techniques to use in school or in the community • Student seeks assistance from teacher	• Adult/peer identifies appropriate listening techniques in the community • Supervisor demonstrates appropriate techniques for listening at training programs or at job placements • Adult/peer demonstrates appropriate techniques for listening while in the community • Student seeks assistance from adult/peer
3. Identify appropriate responding techniques	• Teacher identifies appropriate responding techniques at school and at home • Student lists on chalkboard/chart the appropriate techniques for responding at school and at home • Teacher demonstrates some of the most appropriate responding techniques to use at school and at home • Speaker demonstrates some of the most appropriate responding techniques to use in school or in the community • Student seeks assistance from teacher	• Adult/peer identifies appropriate responding techniques in the community • Supervisor demonstrates appropriate techniques for responding at training programs or at job placements • Adult/peer demonstrates appropriate techniques for responding while in the community • Student seeks assistance from adult/peer
4. Practice attentive listening and responding	• Student develops self-monitoring plan for practicing attentive listening and responding skills in school and at home • Student demonstrates using the skills of attentive listening and responding in school and at home • Student seeks assistance from teacher	• Student develops self-monitoring plan for practicing attentive listening and responding skills in job placements and in the community • Student demonstrates using the skills of attentive listening and responding at job placements and in the community • Student seeks assistance from adult/peer

PERSONAL-SOCIAL SKILLS

Domain: Personal-Social Skills
Competency 14: Communicating with Others
Subcompetency 54: Demonstrate Effective Communication

Objectives	Training Activities	Home-/Community-Based Training Activities
1. Identify modes of communication	• Teacher identifies modes of communication at school and home • Student lists on chalkboard/chart the effective techniques of communication at school and at home • Teacher demonstrates some of the most effective communication techniques to use at school and at home • Guest speaker demonstrates some of the most effective communication techniques to use in school or in the community • Student seeks assistance from teacher	• Adult/peer identifies modes of communication in the community • Supervisor demonstrates appropriate techniques for communicating at training programs or at job placements • Adult/peer demonstrates appropriate techniques for communicating while in the community • Student seeks assistance from adult/peer
2. Identify appropriate speaking methods	• Teacher identifies various appropriate speaking methods used in school or at home • Student discusses why people use different appropriate speaking method in school or at home • Teacher demonstrates appropriate speaking methods at school and home • Student constructs poster outlining some of the appropriate speaking methods used in the school or at home • Student seeks assistance from teacher	• Adult/peer describes appropriate speaking methods he or she uses in training programs or job placements • Adult/peer describes appropriate speaking methods he or she uses in the community • Adult/peer demonstrates appropriate speaking methods in the community • Adult/peer explores the community with student discussing other peoples' speaking methods used appropriately in the community • Student seeks assistance from adult/peer
3. Identify inappropriate speaking methods	• Teacher identifies various inappropriate speaking methods used in school or at home • Student discusses why people use different inappropriate speaking methods in school or at home • Teacher demonstrates inappropriate speaking methods at school and home • Student constructs poster outlining some of the inappropriate speaking methods used in the school or at home • Student seeks assistance from teacher	• Adult/peer describes inappropriate speaking methods used in training programs or job placements • Adult/peer describes inappropriate speaking methods used in the community • Adult/peer demonstrates inappropriate speaking methods in the community • Adult/peer explores the community with student, discussing other peoples' speaking methods used inappropriately in the community • Student seeks assistance from adult/peer
4. Identify methods of expressing needs and feelings	• Student discusses why people express different needs and feelings in school or at home • Teacher identifies various methods of expressing needs and feelings in school or at home • Teacher demonstrates methods of expressing needs and feelings at school and at home	• Adult/peer describes appropriate methods of expression of needs and feelings in training programs or job placements • Adult/peer describes appropriate methods of expression of needs and feelings in the community • Adult/peer demonstrates methods of expressing needs and feelings in the community

PERSONAL-SOCIAL SKILLS

PERSONAL-SOCIAL SKILLS

	Training Activities	Home-/Community-Based Training Activities
	• Student constructs poster outlining some of the most common methods of expression of needs and feelings in the school or at home • Student seeks assistance from teacher	• Adult/peer explores the community with student, discussing methods other people use to express needs and feelings • Student seeks assistance from adult/peer
5. Identify appropriate techniques of communicating on the telephone	• Teacher identifies appropriate techniques of communicating on the telephone at home • Student lists on chalkboard/chart the appropriate techniques for communicating on the telephone at home • Teacher demonstrates some of the most appropriate communication techniques to use on the telephone at home • Representative from local telephone service discusses some of the most appropriate telephone communication techniques to use in school or in the community • Student seeks assistance from teacher	• Adult/peer identifies appropriate techniques of communicating on the telephone in the community • Supervisor demonstrates appropriate techniques for communicating on the telephone at training programs or at job placements • Adult/peer demonstrates appropriate techniques for communicating on the telephone while in the community • Student seeks assistance from adult/peer
6. Identify nonverbal cues and communication skills	• Teacher identifies some of the most appropriate nonverbal communication techniques to use at school and at home • Speaker discusses some of the most appropriate nonverbal communication techniques to use in school or in the community • Student lists on chalkboard/chart the appropriate nonverbal communication techniques to use in school and at home • Student seeks assistance from teacher	• Supervisor discusses appropriate nonverbal communication techniques used at training programs or at job placements • Adult/peer demonstrates appropriate nonverbal communication techniques used in the community • Student seeks assistance from adult/peer
7. Practice effective communication	• Student develops self-monitoring plan for practicing effective communication skills in school and at home • Student demonstrates using the skills of effective communication in school and at home	• Student develops self-monitoring plan practicing effective communication skills in job placements and in the community • Student demonstrates using the skills of effective communication in job placements and in the community

Domain: Personal-Social Skills
Competency 14: Communicating with Others
Subcompetency 55: Communicate in Emergency Situations

Objectives	Training Activities	Home-/Community-Based Training Activities
1. Identify signs of an emergency situation	• Teacher identifies signs indicating an emergency situation in school or at home • Student lists on chalkboard/chart the effective techniques of communicating emergencies at school and at home • Teacher demonstrates some of the most effective communication techniques to use for emergencies at school and at home	• Adult/peer identifies signs indicating an emergency situation in the community • Supervisor demonstrates appropriate techniques for communicating emergencies at training programs or at job placements • Adult/peer demonstrates appropriate techniques for communicating emergencies while in the community

Objectives	Training Activities	Home-/Community-Based Training Activities
	• Guest speaker discusses some of the most effective communication techniques to use use during emergency situations in school or in the community • Student seeks assistance from teacher	• Student seeks assistance from adult/peer
2. Identify appropriate authorities to contact in different emergency situations	• Teacher identifies appropriate authorities to contact in different emergency situations • Student lists on chalkboard/chart appropriate authorities to contact in various emergency situations occurring in school or at home • Teacher discusses some of the more appropriate authorities to contact in various emergency situations occurring in school and at home • Guest speaker discusses some of the more appropriate authorities to contact in various emergency situations occurring in school, at home, or in the community • Student seeks assistance from teacher	• Adult/peer identifies appropriate authorities to contact in different emergency situations • Supervisor discusses various appropriate authorities to contact during emergency situations occurring at training programs or at job placements • Adult/peer discusses various appropriate authorities to contact during emergency situations in the community • Student seeks assistance from adult/peer
3. Practice communicating in emergency situations	• Student develops self-monitoring plan for practicing effective communication skills during emergency situations that occur in school or at home • Student demonstrates using the skills of effective communication during emergency situations in school and at home • Student seeks assistance from teacher	• Student develops self-monitoring plan for practicing effective communication skills during emergency situations occurring in job placements and in the community • Student demonstrates using the skills of effective communication during emergency situations in job placements and in the community • Student seeks assistance from adult/peer

OCCUPATIONAL GUIDANCE AND PREPARATION

Domain: Occupational Guidance and Preparation
Competency 15: Exploring and Locating Occupational Training and Job Placement Opportunities
Subcompetency 56: Identify Rewards of Working

Objectives	Training Activities	Home-/Community-Based Training Activities
1. Identify the importance of working	• Teacher discusses importance of working at school and home • Student discusses the reasons for paid and unpaid work. • Student seeks assistance from teacher	• Adult/peer discusses importance of working in the community • Adult/peer discusses reasons he or she works • Student seeks assistance from adult/peer
2. Discuss the rewards of working	• Teacher discusses the rewards of working at school and home • Student develops collage illustrating material rewards of working • Student discusses nonmaterial rewards of working • Student seeks assistance from teacher	• Adult/peer discusses the rewards of working in the community • Student writes out list of material rewards of working • Student writes out list of nonmaterial rewards of working • Student seeks assistance from adult/peer
3. Identify the reasons some jobs pay more than others	• Teacher discusses the reasons why some jobs pay more than others	• Adult/peer discusses the reasons why some jobs pay more than others in the community

OCCUPATIONAL GUIDANCE
AND PREPARATION

	• Student discusses different jobs that are available in the community • Student discusses the jobs that pay the most and least • Student seeks assistance from teacher	• Student describes different jobs that are available in the community • Student explores the reasons for pay differentials among jobs • Student seeks assistance from adult/peer
4. Identify personal needs that are met through work	• Teacher discusses how personal needs are met through work • Student states personal needs for working • Student develops collage of personal needs that are met through work • Student seeks assistance from teacher	• Adult/peer discusses how personal needs met through work • Student writes out list of personal needs for working • Student discusses personal needs that are met through work with adult/peer • Student seeks assistance from adult/peer
5. Identify how work is part of one's personal identity	• Teacher discusses how work is part of one's personal identity • Student discusses how work is part of one's parents'/guardians' identity • Student seeks assistance from teacher	• Adult/peer discusses how work is part of one's personal identity • Student explores identity gained through work • Student seeks assistance from adult/peer
6. Identify ways workers contribute to society	• Teacher discusses how workers contribute to society • Student discusses how working benefits the community • Student seeks assistance from teacher	• Adult/peer discusses how workers contribute to society • Student demonstrates how working benefits society • Student seeks assistance from adult/peer
7. Identify ways society rewards different types of jobs	• Teacher discusses ways society rewards different types of jobs • Student states how the community rewards workers • Student seeks assistance from teacher	• Adult/peer discusses ways society rewards different types of jobs • Student explores how the community rewards workers • Student seeks assistance from adult/peer

Domain: Occupational Guidance and Preparation
Competency 15: Exploring and Locating Occupational Training and Job Placement Opportunities
Subcompetency 57: Locate Available Occupational Training and Job Placement Possibilities

Objectives	Training Activities	Home-/Community-Based Training Activities
1. Identify sources for locating occupational training and job placement information	• Teacher identifies sources for locating occupational training and job placements • Student visits job service office and lists job sources' agencies • Student states community agencies providing information regarding job placement and occupational training opportunities • Student seeks assistance from teacher	• Adult/peer identifies sources for locating occupational training and job placements • Student visits job service office and lists job sources' agencies • Student writes out list of information needed for job placement and training opportunities • Student seeks assistance from adult/peer
2. Discuss different types of occupational training possibilities	• Teacher identifies possible occupational training placements • Student identifies possible community occupational training sites • Student seeks assistance from teacher	• Adult/peer identifies possible occupational training placements • Student locates possible community occupational training sites • Student seeks assistance from adult/peer

3. Identify general job placement possibilities	• Teacher identifies possible job placements • Student states potential jobs in the community • Student seeks assistance from teacher	• Adult/peer identifies possible job placements • Student determines potential jobs in the community • Student seeks assistance from adult/peer
4. Identify general training possibilities	• Teacher identifies general training possibilities • Student states potential occupational training options • Student seeks assistance from teacher	• Adult/peer identifies general training possibilities • Student describes potential occupational training options • Student seeks assistance from adult/peer
5. Practice locating available occupational training possibilities	• Student locates community occupational training options • Student locates community job options by role playing • Student seeks assistance from teacher	• Student demonstrates community job options, by example • Student locates available occupational training possibilities with adult/peer • Student seeks assistance from adult/peer
6. Request assistance for locating occupational training possibilities	• Student identifies whom to request help from in locating community occupational training and job placement possibilities • Student role plays locating sources for helping to find community occupational training and job placement possibilities • Student requests help locating occupational training options	• Student locates sources for assistance in community occupational training and job placement possibilities • Student locates sources for occupational training options

Domain: Occupational Guidance and Preparation
Competency 16: Making Occupational Training and Job Placement Choices
Subcompetency 58: Demonstrate Knowledge of Occupational Interests

Objectives	Training Activities	Home-/Community-Based Training Activities
1. Identify occupational interests	• Teacher identifies personal occupational interests and examples of other people's occupational interests • Student discusses job interests and teacher lists on chalkboard • Student seeks assistance from teacher	• Adult/peer identifies personal occupational interests and examples of other peoples' occupational interests • Student describes jobs that are of interest to adult/peer • Student seeks assistance from adult/peer
2. Discuss types of jobs matching personal occupational interests	• Student develops collage identifying jobs matching personal occupational interests • Student presents collage to other students and discusses jobs that are available in the community • Student seeks assistance from teacher	• Student writes out list of jobs matching personal occupational interests • Student writes out list of available jobs in community and discusses with adult/peer • Student seeks assistance from adult/peer
3. Request assistance regarding matching jobs with personal occupational interests	• Student states sources to help to identify realistic occupational training and job choices that match interests • Student role plays seeking help for matching jobs with personal occupational interests • Student requests help in matching jobs with personal occupational interests	• Student determines interests and possible job choices and realistic occupational training that matches • Student requests help from sources that will match jobs and occupational training

OCCUPATIONAL GUIDANCE AND PREPARATION

Domain: Occupational Guidance and Preparation
Competency 16: Making Occupational Training and Job Placement Choices
Subcompetency 59: Demonstrate Knowledge of Occupational Strengths and Weaknesses

Objectives	Training Activities	Home-/Community-Based Training Activities
1. Identify occupational strengths and weaknesses	• Teacher identifies personal occupational strengths and weaknesses and other people's strengths and weaknesses • Student states personal occupational strengths • Student states personal occupational weaknesses • Student seeks assistance from teacher	• Adult/peer identifies personal occupational strengths and weaknesses and other peoples' strengths and weaknesses • Student writes out personal occupational strengths and discusses with adult/peer • Student writes out personal occupational weaknesses and discusses with adult/peer • Student seeks assistance from adult/peer
2. Discuss jobs matching personal occupational strengths	• Teacher meets with student and discusses job requirements of jobs matching personal occupational strengths and interests • Student develops collage of jobs matching personal occupational strengths • Student seeks assistance from teacher	• Adult/peer meets with student and discusses job requirements of jobs matching personal occupational strengths and interests • Student writes out occupational strengths and discusses jobs matching strengths with adult/peer • Student seeks assistance from adult/peer
3. Request assistance regarding matching jobs with personal occupational strengths	• Student identifies sources for helping to match jobs with personal occupational strengths • Student role plays seeking sources for helping to match jobs with personal occupational strengths • Student requests help in matching jobs with personal occupational strengths	• Student assists other student in determining personal occupational strengths and matching with jobs • Student requests help from other sources in matching jobs with personal occupational strengths

Domain: Occupational Guidance and Preparation
Competency 16: Making Occupational Training and Job Placement Choices
Subcompetency 60: Identify Possible and Available Jobs Matching Interests and Strengths

Objectives	Training Activities	Home-/Community-Based Training Activities
1. Identify jobs of interest	• Student looks through catalogs and identifies jobs of interest • Student lists jobs of interest on chart/poster • Student develops collage of jobs of interest	• Student discusses with adult/peer jobs that are of interest • Student writes out list of jobs of interest and discusses with adult/peer
2. State jobs of interest that match personal occupational strengths and weaknesses	• Student lists jobs of interest that match personal occupational strengths and weaknesses • Student lists jobs of interest on chart/poster • Student develops collage of jobs of interest	• Student writes out list of jobs of interest that match personal occupational strengths and weaknesses • Student writes out list of jobs of interest and discusses with adult/peer
3. Discuss job-related requirements of jobs matching personal occupational interests	• Teacher meets with student and discusses job requirements of jobs matching personal occupational strengths and interests	• Adult/peer meets with student and discusses job requirements of jobs matching personal occupational strengths and interests

OCCUPATIONAL GUIDANCE AND PREPARATION

• Student states general job requirements • Student identifies the job-related requirements of jobs matching personal occupational interests • Student seeks assistance from teacher	• Student demonstrates an understanding of the general job requirements • Student finds out more about the jobs that match her/his personal occupational interests from other sources • Student seeks assistance from adult/peer

Domain: Occupational Guidance and Preparation
Competency 16: Making Occupational Training and Job Placement Choices
Subcompetency 61: Plan and Make Realistic Occupational Training and Job Placement Decisions

Objectives	Training Activities	Home-/Community-Based Training Activities
1. Identify occupational training and job placement options	• Teacher identifies student's occupational training and job placement options • Student lists occupational training and/or job placement possibilities • Student seeks assistance from teacher	• Adult/peer identifies student's occupational training and job placement options • Student demonstrates an understanding of the occupational training and job placement possibilities • Student seeks assistance from adult/peer
2. Develop plan to meet identified occupational training and job placement options	• Teacher meets with student and discusses developing plan for meeting identified occupational training and job placements • Student devises a plan outlining realistic occupational training and/or job placement possibilities • Student seeks assistance from teacher	• Adult/peer meets with student and discusses developing plan for meeting identified occupational training and job placements • Student writes out a plan outlining realistic occupational training and job placement possibilities • Student seeks assistance from adult/peer
3. Request assistance to help plan and make realistic occupational training and job placement choices	• Teacher identifies sources of assistance for helping to plan and make realistic occupational training and job placement choices • Student states sources to help him/her plan and make realistic occupational training and job placement decisions and list them on poster/chart • Student role plays seeking help in planning and making realistic occupational training and job placement decisions • Student requests help to plan and make realistic occupational training and job placement decisions	• Adult/peer identifies sources of assistance for helping to plan and make realistic occupational training and job placement choices • Student demonstrates an understanding of seeking help in planning and making realistic occupational training and job placement decisions • Student requests help in planning and making realistic occupational training and job placement decisions

Domain: Occupational Guidance and Preparation
Competency 16: Making Occupational Training and Job Placement Choices
Subcompetency 62: Develop Training Plan for Occupational Choice

Objectives	Training Activities	Home-/Community-Based Training Activities
1. Identify steps in developing occupational choice training plan	• Teacher meets with student and discusses steps in developing occupational choice training plan • Student devises steps for developing occupational choice training plan • Student seeks assistance from teacher	• Adult/peer meets with student and discusses steps in developing occupational choice training plan • Student writes out steps for developing an occupational choice training plan • Student seeks assistance from adult/peer

OCCUPATIONAL GUIDANCE AND PREPARATION

2. Develop occupational choice training plan	• Teacher meets with student and discusses developing occupational choice training plan • Student devises an occupational choice training plan • Student seeks assistance from teacher	• Adult/peer meets with student and discusses developing occupational choice training plan • Student writes out an occupational choice training plan • Student seeks assistance from adult/peer

Domain: Occupational Guidance and Preparation
Competency 17: Applying for and Maintaining Occupational Training and Job Placements
Subcompetency 63: Apply for Occupational Training and Job Placement

Objectives	Training Activities	Home-/Community-Based Training Activities
1. Identify steps in applying for occupational training and job placements	• Human resources manager (HRM) identifies the steps in applying for occupational training and job placements • Student discusses steps in applying for occupational training and job placements • Student role plays steps in applying for occupational training and job placements • Student seeks assistance from teacher	• Student visits human resources office and manager identifies the steps in applying for occupational training and job placements • Student demonstrates an understanding of the steps in applying for occupational training and job placements • Student seeks assistance from adult/peer
2. Collect and develop personal data card for completing application forms	• Teacher meets with student and discusses developing personal data card or completing job application forms • Student states personal information generally included on most job applications and lists on chart/poster • Student pairs present to each other personal data that is generally included on most applications and they add other information on chart/poster • Student develops personal data card for use when completing application forms • Student seeks assistance from teacher	• Adult/peer meets with student and discusses developing personal data card or completing job applications • Student brings personal data generally included on most applications to adult/peer and they work on developing personal data form • Student writes out on card the personal data used when completing application forms • Student presents personal data form to an HRM and asks him/her to review and make suggestions for revisions • Student seeks assistance from adult/peer
3. Complete applications for occupational training and job placements	• Human resources manager identifies the steps in applying for occupational training and job placements • Student discusses items on several occupational training and job applications and teacher reviews • Student pairs complete several occupational training and job applications • Student demonstrates how to complete occupational training and job applications with teacher • Student completes several examples of occupational training and job applications • Student seeks assistance from teacher	• Student visits human resources office and officer identifies the steps in applying for occupational training and job placements • Student completes several occupational training and job applications and has HRM review • Student reviews HR office's occupational training and job applications • Student completes several examples of occupational training and job applications and reviews with adult/peer • Student completes job applications in HR office using personal data form • Student seeks assistance from adult/peer
4. Request assistance in applying for occupational training and/or job placement	• HRM demonstrates sources for assisting in applying for occupational training and/or job placements • Student states how to seek help in completing occupational training and/or job applications	• HRM discusses sources for assisting in applying for occupational training and/or job placements • Student demonstrates an understanding of seeking help in completing occupational training and job applications

OCCUPATIONAL GUIDANCE AND PREPARATION

	• Student role plays seeking help in completing occupational training and/or job applications • Student requests help in completing occupational training and/or job applications • Student seeks assistance from teacher	• Student requests help in completing occupational training and job applications • Student seeks assistance from HRM in completing occupational training and/or job applications • Student seeks assistance from adult/peer

Domain: Occupational Guidance and Preparation
Competency 17: Applying for and Maintaining Occupational Training and Job Placements
Subcompetency 64: Interview for Occupational Training and Job Placements

Objectives	Training Activities	Home-/Community-Based Training Activities
1. Identify appropriate interview skills for occupational training and job placements	• Student visits business/agency HRM to learn about interviewing practices • Student states appropriate interview practices to another student • Student states inappropriate interview practices to another student • Student develops poster/chart listing appropriate interview skills • Student seeks assistance from teacher	• Student visits business/agency HRM to learn about interviewing practices • Student demonstrates an understanding of appropriate interview practices with adult/peer • Student states inappropriate interview practices to adult/peer • Student writes the appropriate interview skills • Student seeks assistance from adult/peer
2. Practice mock interviews for occupational training and job placements	• Student visits business/agency and practices mock interviewing with HR department • Student pairs practices mock interviews with each other and critique each others' interviews • Student seeks assistance from teacher	• Student visits business/agency and participates in mock interviews with HR department • Student practices mock interviews with adult/peer and critiques interview • Student seeks assistance from adult/peer
3. Practice interviews for occupational training and job placements	• Student visits business/agency and practices interviewing with HR department • Student pairs practice interviewing with each other and critique each others' interview • Student seeks assistance from teacher	• Student visits business/agency and participates in interviews with HR department • Student practices interviews with adult/peer and critiques interview • Student seeks assistance from adult/peer
4. Request help in preparing and interviewing for occupational training and job placements	• HRM demonstrates sources for assistance in preparing for occupational training and/or job placement interviews • Student identifies sources for helping in preparing and interviewing for occupational training and job placements • Student role plays seeking help in preparing and interviewing for occupational training and job placements • Student states how to seek help in preparing and interviewing for occupational training and/or job placements • Student requests help for preparing and interviewing for occupational training and job placements • Student seeks assistance from teacher	• HRM demonstrates sources for assistance in preparing for occupational training and/or job placement interviews • Student demonstrates an understanding of seeking help in preparing and interviewing for occupational training and job placements in the community • Student requests assistance in preparing and interviewing for occupational training and job placements with an agency • Student demonstrates an understanding of seeking help in preparing and interviewing for occupational training and job placements • Student seeks assistance from personnel officer preparing for and interviewing for occupational training and job placements • Student seeks assistance from adult/peer

OCCUPATIONAL GUIDANCE AND PREPARATION

Domain: Occupational Guidance and Preparation
Competency 17: Applying for and Maintaining Occupational Training and Job Placements
Subcompetency 65: Make Adjustments to Changes in Employment Status

Objectives	Training Activities	Home-/Community-Based Training Activities
1. Identify potential problems encountered in occupational training and job placements	• HRM discusses potential problems encountered in occupational training job placements • Student visits business/agency HRM to learn of potential problems to be encountered while participating in occupational training and in jobs • Student discusses problems that may be encountered while participating in occupational training and maintaining a job with teacher • Student role plays potential problems that may be encountered while participating in occupational training and maintaining a job • Student seeks assistance from teacher	• HRM discusses potential problems encountered in occupational training and job placements • Student visits business/agency HRM and asks him/her what problems may be encountered while participating in occupational training and maintaining a job • Student makes a list of different problems that may be encountered while participating in occupational training and maintaining a job • Student discusses with adult/peer potential problems that may be encountered while participating in occupational training and maintaining a job • Student seeks assistance from adult/peer
2. Identify potential solutions to problems encountered in occupational training and job placements	• HRM discusses potential solutions to problems encountered in occupational training and job placements • Student visits business/agency HRM to learn of solutions to potential problems to be encountered while participating in occupational training and in jobs • Student discusses with teacher problems that may be encountered while participating in occupational training and maintaining a job • Student role plays potential solutions to problems that may be encountered while participating in occupational training and maintaining a job • Student seeks assistance from teacher	• HRM discusses potential solutions to problems encountered in occupational training and job placements • Student visits business/agency HRM and asks him/her what are some solutions to problems encountered while participating in occupational training and maintaining a job • Student makes a list of different solutions to problems that may be encountered while participating in occupational training and maintaining a job • Student discusses with adult/peer potential solutions to problems that may be encountered while participating in occupational training and maintaining a job • Student seeks assistance from adult/peer
3. Identify factors that determine successful work adjustment	• Student discusses successful work adjustment skills (e.g., getting along with co-workers, taking appropriate time for lunch and breaks, etc.) • HRM discusses potential factors in successful work adjustment • Student visits business/agency HRM to learn of potential factors that determine successful work adjustment • Student discusses factors determining successful work adjustment with teacher • Student role plays potential factors that determine successful work adjustment • Student seeks assistance from teacher	• Students, in pairs, develop a list of successful work adjustment skills for occupational training and jobs and review list with HRM • Personnel officer discusses potential factors in successful work adjustment • Student visits business/agency HRM and asks him/her what factors determine successful work adjustment • Student makes a list of factors determining successful work adjustment with adult/peer • Student discusses potential factors that determine successful work adjustment • Student seeks assistance from adult/peer

OCCUPATIONAL GUIDANCE AND PREPARATION

4. Identify factors that determine unsuccessful work adjustment	• Student discusses unsuccessful work adjustment skills (e.g., inability to get along with coworkers, taking inappropriate time for lunch and breaks, etc.) • HRM discusses potential factors in unsuccessful work adjustment • Student visits business/agency HRM to learn of potential factors that determine unsuccessful work adjustment • Student discusses factors determining unsuccessful work adjustment with teacher • Student role plays potential factors that determine unsuccessful work adjustment • Student seeks assistance from teacher	• Student pairs develop a list of unsuccessful work adjustment skills for occupational training and jobs and review list with HRM • HRM discusses potential factors in unsuccessful work adjustment • Student visits business/agency HRM and asks him/her what factors determine unsuccessful work adjustment • Student makes a list of factors determining unsuccessful work adjustment with adult/peer • Student discusses potential factors that determine unsuccessful work adjustment • Student seeks assistance from adult/peer
5. Identify reasons for occupational training or employment changes or termination	• HRM discusses reasons for employment changes or termination • Student role plays scenarios depicting reasons employees lose jobs or change place of employment • Student develops list of reasons why employees lose jobs or change place of employment • Student seeks assistance from teacher	• Student speaks with HRM about reasons for employment changes or termination • Student provides, to adult/peer, five factors related to being terminated and five factors related to why employees decide to change jobs/training programs • Student discusses reasons with personnel officer why employees lose jobs or change place of employment • Student seeks assistance from adult/peer
6. Identify factors relating to being promoted in jobs	• Student discusses factors related to being promoted in jobs • HRM discusses factors related to being promoted in jobs • Student visits business/agency HRM to learn of potential factors related to being promoted in jobs • Student discusses factors related to being promoted in jobs with teacher • Student role plays potential factors that are related to being promoted in jobs • Student seeks assistance from teacher	• Student pairs discuss factors related to being promoted in jobs • HRM discusses factors related to being promoted in jobs • Student visits business/agency HRM and asks him/her what factors are related to being promoted in jobs • Student makes a list of factors related to being promoted in jobs with adult/peer • Student discusses potential factors that are related to being promoted in jobs • Student seeks assistance from adult/peer
7. Request assistance in making changes in employment status	• HRM discusses sources for assistance in making changes in employment status • Student identifies sources for helping in making changes in employment status • Student role plays seeking help in making changes in employment status • Student states how to seek help in making changes in employment status • Student requests help in making changes in employment status • Student seeks assistance from teacher	• HRM discusses sources for assistance in making changes in employment status • Student demonstrates an understanding of seeking help in making changes in employment status • Student requests assistance in making changes in employment status • Student demonstrates an understanding of seeking help in making changes in employment status • Student seeks assistance from personnel officer in making changes in employment status • Student seeks assistance from adult/peer

Domain: Occupational Guidance and Preparation
Competency 18: Developing and Maintaining Appropriate Work Skills and Behavior
Subcompetency 66: Perform Work Directions and Meet Requirements

Objectives	Training Activities	Home-/Community-Based Training Activities
1. Identify the importance of following directions and meeting requirements	• Teacher discusses importance of following authorities' directions/instructions in jobs • Student lists on chalkboard/chart the importance of following authorities' directions at jobs	• Adult/peer discusses importance of following authorities' directions/instructions in jobs • Supervisor discusses the importance of following authorities' directions/instructions in training programs or job placements
2. Perform a series of tasks in response to verbal instructions	• Student practices completing a series of work/job tasks with partner after receiving verbal instructions • Student practices completing a series of work/job tasks alone after receiving verbal instructions	• Student completes a series of tasks in the community with a partner after receiving verbal instructions • Student completes a series of tasks in the community alone after receiving verbal instructions

Domain: Occupational Guidance and Preparation
Competency 18: Developing and Maintaining Appropriate Work Skills and Behavior
Subcompetency 67: Maintain Good Attendance and Punctuality

Objectives	Training Activities	Home-/Community-Based Training Activities
1. Identify reasons for good attendance and punctuality	• HRM discusses reasons for good attendance and punctuality at occupational training and job placements • Student role plays scenarios depicting reason for good attendance and punctuality in occupational training and job placements • Student develops list of reasons why it is important to have good attendance and punctuality in occupational training and job placements • Student seeks assistance from teacher	• Student speaks with HRM about reasons for good attendance and punctuality at occupational training and job placements • Student provides five reasons for good attendance and punctuality in occupational training and job placements with adult/peer • Student discusses reasons why it is important to have good attendance and punctuality at occupational training and job placements with HRM • Student seeks assistance from adult/peer
2. Identify actions to take for tardiness or absence from work	• HRM discusses appropriate actions to take for tardiness or absence from work • Student role plays scenarios depicting actions to take for tardiness or absence from work • Student develops list of actions to take for tardiness or absence from work • Student seeks assistance from teacher	• Student speaks with HRM about actions to take for tardiness or absence from work • Student provides five actions to take for tardiness or absence from work • Student demonstrates actions to take for tardiness or absence from work • Student seeks assistance from adult/peer

Domain: Occupational Guidance and Preparation
Competency 18: Developing and Maintaining Appropriate Work Skills and Behavior
Subcompetency 68: Respond Appropriately to Supervision

Objectives	Training Activities	Home-/Community-Based Training Activities
1. Identify appropriate behavior when being supervised	• Teacher demonstrates appropriate behavior when being supervised	• Adult/peer demonstrates appropriate behavior when being supervised

OCCUPATIONAL GUIDANCE AND PREPARATION

	• Student lists on chalkboard/chart appropriate behavior when being supervised • Student pairs demonstrate appropriate behavior when being supervised • Student seeks assistance from teacher	• Supervisor demonstrates the importance of appropriate behavior when being supervised • Student demonstrates with adult/peer the importance of appropriate behavior when being supervised • Student seeks assistance from adult/peer
2. Exhibit appropriate response to supervision	• Student practices with partner performing appropriate response to supervision • Student seeks assistance from teacher	• Student performs appropriate response to supervision in community with a partner • Student seeks assistance from adult/peer

Domain: Occupational Guidance and Preparation
Competency 18: Developing and Maintaining Appropriate Work Skills and Behavior
Subcompetency 69: Demonstrate Job Safety

Objectives	Training Activities	Home-/Community-Based Training Activities
1. Identify the importance of job safety	• Teacher discusses importance of following job safety guidelines in occupational training and job placements • Student lists on chalkboard/chart the importance of following job safety guidelines in occupational training and job placements • Student pairs discuss the importance of following job safety guidelines in occupational training and job placements • Student seeks assistance from teacher	• Adult/peer discusses importance of following job safety guidelines in occupational training and job placements • Supervisor discusses the importance of following job safety guidelines in occupational and job placements • Student discusses the importance of following job safety guidelines in occupational training and job placements • Student seeks assistance from adult/peer
2. Identify potential job hazards	• Business supervisor discusses potential job hazards • Student pairs demonstrate the activities that are unsafe/hazardous at an occupational training or job placement • Student demonstrates potential job hazards with teacher • Student develops job hazards poster/chart • Student demonstrates whom to contact when hazardous situations are encountered • Student seeks assistance from teacher	• Business supervisor discusses potential job hazards • Student lists activities that are unsafe or hazardous at occupational training or job placements • Student at job site identifies activities that are unsafe or hazards on the job with adult/peer • Student lists with partner ways to avoid hazards on the job • Student, with adult/peer, explores and lists emergency procedures when hazardous situations are encountered on job site • Student seeks assistance from adult/peer
3. Identify safety measures in job choices	• Business supervisor discusses potential safety measures at job site • Student pairs demonstrate the activities that are safety measures at occupational training or job placements • Student discusses potential job safety measures with teacher • Student develops job safety measures on the job poster/chart • Student demonstrates whom to contact when needing assistance in practicing job safety measures on the job • Student seeks assistance from teacher	• Business supervisor discusses potential safety measures at job site • Student lists activities that are safety measures at occupational training or job placements • Student at job site identifies with adult/peer activities that are safety measures on the job • Student lists with partner ways to practice job safety measures on the job • Student explores and lists job safety measures on job sites with adult/peer • Student seeks assistance from adult/peer

4. Exhibit job safety	• Student practices with partner performing appropriate job safety behaviors • Student seeks assistance from teacher	• Student performs appropriate job safety behaviors in community with a partner • Student seeks assistance from adult/peer

Domain: Occupational Guidance and Preparation
Competency 18: Developing and Maintaining Appropriate Work Skills and Behavior
Subcompetency 70: Work Cooperatively with Others

Objectives	Training Activities	Home-/Community-Based Training Activities
1. Identify reasons for working with others	• HRM discusses reasons for working cooperatively with others at occupational training and job placements • Student role plays scenarios depicting reasons for working cooperatively at occupational training and job placements • Student develops list of reasons why it is important to work cooperatively with others in occupational training and job placements • Student develops poster/chart listing reasons for working cooperatively with others in occupational training and job placements • Student seeks assistance from teacher	• Student speaks with HRM about reasons for working cooperatively with others at occupational training and job placements • Student provides, with adult/peer, five reasons for working cooperatively with others at occupational training and job placements • Student discusses with personnel officer reasons why it is important to work cooperatively with others at occupational training and job placements • Student discusses with adult/peer reasons for working cooperatively with others at occupational training and job placements • Student seeks assistance from adult/peer
2. Practice working cooperatively with others	• Student pairs demonstrate how to work cooperatively with others • Student role plays situations requiring the cooperation of coworkers • Student discusses what actions to take when problems between coworkers occur • Student practices working cooperatively with coworkers • Student seeks assistance from teacher	• Student lists situations that require working cooperatively with others • Student lists appropriate actions to take when problems between coworkers occur • Student works cooperatively with coworkers on job site • Student practices working cooperatively with others while being reviewed by adult/peer • Student seeks assistance from adult/peer

Domain: Occupational Guidance and Preparation
Competency 18: Developing and Maintaining Appropriate Work Skills and Behavior
Subcompetency 71: Meet Work Quality and Quantity Standards

Objectives	Training Activities	Home-/Community-Based Training Activities
1. Identify reasons for work quality standards	• HRM discusses reasons for performing to meet work quality standards at occupational training and job placements ments • Student role plays scenarios depicting reasons for performing to meet work quality standards at occupational training and job placements	• Student speaks with HRM about reasons for performing to meet work quality standards at occupational training and job placements • Student provides, with adult/peer, five reasons for performing to meet work quality standards at occupational training and job placements

	• Student develops list of reasons why it is important to perform to meet work quality standards in occupational training and job placements • Student develops poster/chart listing reasons for performing to meet work quality standards in occupational training and job placements • Student seeks assistance from teacher	• Student discusses with HRM reasons why it is important to perform to meet work quality standards at occupational training and job placements • Student discusses with adult/peer reasons for performing to meet work quality standards at occupational training and job placements • Student seeks assistance from adult/peer
2. Identify reasons for work quantity standards	• HRM discusses reasons for performing to meet work quantity standards at occupational training and job placements • Student role plays scenarios depicting reasons for performing to meet work quantity standards in occupational training and job placements • Student develops list of reasons why it is important to perform to meet work quantity standards in occupational training and job placements • Student develops poster/chart listing reasons for performing to meet work quantity standards in occupational training and job placements • Student seeks assistance from teacher	• Student speaks with HRM about reasons for performing to meet work quantity standards at occupational training and job placements • Student provides, with adult/peer, five reasons for performing to meet work quantity standards at occupational training and job placements • Student discusses with HRM reasons why it is important to perform to meet work quantity standards at occupational training and job placements • Student discusses with adult/peer reasons for performing to meet work quantity standards at occupational training and job placements • Student seeks assistance from adult/peer
3. Identify consequences of not meeting work quality and quantity standards	• Business supervisor discusses the consequences of not meeting work quality and quantity standards at occupational training and job placements • Student discusses the consequences of not meeting work quality and quantity standards at occupational training and job placements • Teacher discusses the consequences of not meeting work quality and quantity standards at occupational training and job placements • Student seeks assistance from teacher	• Student visits business and supervisor discusses the consequences of not meeting work quality and quantity standards at occupational training and job placements • Student lists the consequences of not meeting work quality and quantity standards at occupational training and job placements • Student visits work site, interviews employers, and discusses the consequences of not meeting work standards at occupational training and job placements • Student seeks assistance from adult/peer
4. Practice meeting work quality and quantity standards	• Student pairs discuss how to meet work quality and quantity standards • Student role plays situations meeting work quality and quantity standards • Student demonstrates what actions to take to meet work quality and quantity standards • Student practices working to meet work quality and quantity standards • Student seeks assistance from teacher	• Student practices meeting work quality and quantity standards • Student lists appropriate actions to take to meet work quality and quantity standards • Student works at meeting work quality and quantity standards on job site with supervisor • Student practices working to meet work quality and quantity standards with co-worker • Student seeks assistance from adult/peer

OCCUPATIONAL GUIDANCE AND PREPARATION

Domain: Occupational Guidance and Preparation
Competency 19: Matching Physical/Manual Skills to Occupational Training and Employment
Subcompetency 72: Demonstrate Fine Motor Dexterity in Occupational Training and Job Placements

Objectives	Training Activities	Home-/Community-Based Training Activities
1. Identify need for good fine motor dexterity in occupational training and employment	• HRM discusses reasons for good fine motor dexterity in occupational training and job placements • Student role plays scenarios depicting reasons for exhibiting good fine motor dexterity in occupational training and job placements • Student develops list of reasons why good fine motor dexterity is important at occupational training and job placements • Student develops poster/chart listing reasons for exhibiting good fine motor dexterity at occupational training and job placements • Student seeks assistance from teacher	• Student speaks with HRM about reasons for good fine motor dexterity in occupational training and job placements • Student provides, with adult/peer, five reasons for exhibiting good fine motor dexterity at occupational training and job placements • Student discusses with HRM reasons why good fine motor dexterity is important at occupational training and job placements • Student discusses with adult/peer reasons for exhibiting good fine motor dexterity at occupational training and job placements • Student seeks assistance from adult/peer
2. Identify jobs in which fine motor dexterity is critical	• Student develops a list of jobs requiring good fine motor dexterity • Guest speaker discusses the many jobs requiring good fine motor dexterity • Student develops poster identifying 20 jobs requiring good fine motor dexterity • Student seeks assistance from teacher	• Student visits jobs that require good fine motor dexterity • Student visits several job sites and identifies the jobs that require good fine motor dexterity • Student discusses with adult/peer several jobs that require good fine motor dexterity • Student seeks assistance from adult/peer
3. Demonstrate fine motor dexterity in occupational training programs and/or at job sites	• Student pairs demonstrate how to perform good fine motor dexterity at occupational training and job placements • Student role plays situations demonstrating good fine motor dexterity • Student demonstrates what actions to take to perform good fine motor dexterity at occupational training and job placements • Student practices working to perform good fine motor dexterity at occupational training and job placements • Student seeks assistance from teacher	• Student practices demonstrating good fine motor dexterity at occupational training and job placements • Student lists appropriate actions to take to demonstrate good fine motor dexterity at occupational training and job placements • Student works at demonstrating good fine motor dexterity on job site with supervisor • Student practices working to meet good fine motor dexterity with coworker • Student seeks assistance from adult/peer
4. Request assistance in developing fine motor dexterity in occupational training and job placements	• HRM discusses sources for assistance in developing good fine motor dexterity • Student identifies to teacher sources for help in developing good fine motor dexterity • Student role plays seeking help to improve fine motor dexterity • Student states how to seek help in improving fine motor dexterity • Student requests help for making improvements in fine motor dexterity • Student seeks assistance from teacher	• HRM discusses sources for assistance in developing good fine motor dexterity • Student demonstrates an understanding of seeking help in developing good fine motor dexterity • Student requests assistance in developing good fine motor dexterity • Student demonstrates an understanding of seeking help to improve fine motor dexterity • Student seeks assistance from personnel officer for developing good fine motor dexterity • Student seeks assistance from adult/peer

OCCUPATIONAL GUIDANCE AND PREPARATION

Domain: Occupational Guidance and Preparation
Competency 19: Matching Physical/Manual Skills to Occupational Training and Employment
Subcompetency 73: Demonstrate Gross Motor Dexterity in Occupational Training and Job Placements

Objectives	Training Activities	Home-/Community-Based Training Activities
1. Identify need for gross motor dexterity in occupational training and employment	• HRM discusses reasons for good gross motor dexterity in occupational training and job placements • Student role plays scenarios depicting reasons for demonstrating good gross motor dexterity at occupational training and job placements • Student develops list of reasons why good gross motor dexterity is important at occupational training and job placements • Student develops poster/chart listing reasons for having good gross motor dexterity at occupational training and job placements • Student seeks assistance from teacher	• Student speaks with HRM about reasons for good gross motor dexterity in occupational training and job placements • Student provides, with adult/peer, five reasons for demonstrating good gross motor dexterity at occupational training and job placements • Student discusses with personnel officer reasons why it is important to have good gross motor dexterity at occupational training and job placements • Student discusses with adult/peer reasons for having good gross motor dexterity at occupational training and job placements • Student seeks assistance from adult/peer
2. Identify jobs in which gross motor dexterity is critical	• Student develops a list of jobs requiring good gross motor dexterity • Guest speaker discusses the many jobs requiring good gross motor dexterity • Student develops poster identifying 20 jobs requiring good gross motor dexterity • Student seeks assistance from teacher	• Student visits jobs that require good gross motor dexterity • Student visits several job sites and identifies the jobs that require good gross motor dexterity • Student discusses with adult/peer several jobs that require good gross motor dexterity • Student seeks assistance from adult/peer
3. Demonstrate gross motor dexterity in occupational training programs and/or at job sites	• Student pairs demonstrate how to exhibit good gross motor dexterity at occupational training and job placements • Student role plays situations exhibiting good gross motor dexterity • Student discusses what actions to take to exhibit good gross motor dexterity at occupational training and job placements • Student practices working to exhibit good gross motor dexterity at occupational training and job placements • Student seeks assistance from teacher	• Student practices exhibiting good gross motor dexterity at occupational training and job placements • Student lists appropriate actions to take to exhibit good gross motor dexterity at occupational training and job placements • Student works at meeting good gross motor dexterity requirements on job site with supervisor • Student practices working to meet good gross motor dexterity requirements with coworker • Student seeks assistance from adult/peer
4. Request assistance in developing gross motor dexterity in occupational training and job placements	• HRM discusses sources for assistance in developing good gross motor dexterity • Student identifies to teacher sources for help in developing good gross motor dexterity • Student role plays seeking help to improve gross motor dexterity • Student states how to seek help in improving gross motor dexterity • Student requests help for making improvements in gross motor dexterity • Student seeks assistance from teacher	• HRM discusses sources for assistance in developing good gross motor dexterity • Student demonstrates an understanding of seeking help to improve gross motor dexterity • Student requests assistance in developing good gross motor dexterity • Student demonstrates an understanding of seeking help in developing good gross motor dexterity • Student seeks assistance from HRM for for developing good gross motor dexterity

OCCUPATIONAL GUIDANCE AND PREPARATION

Domain: Occupational Guidance and Preparation
Competency 19: Matching Physical/Manual Skills to Occupational Training and Employment
Subcompetency 74: Demonstrate Sensory Discrimination in Occupational Training and Job Placements

Objectives	*Training Activities*	*Home-/Community-Based Training Activities*
1. Demonstrate size and shape discrimination	• Student pairs demonstrate how to perform size and shape discrimination at occupational training and job placements • Student role plays performing in situations where size and shape discrimination is required • Student discusses what actions to take to perform size and shape discrimination tasks at occupational training and job placements • Student practices working to perform size and shape discrimination tasks at occupational training and job placements • Student seeks assistance from teacher	• Student practices performing size and shape discrimination tasks at occupational training and job placements • Student lists appropriate actions to take to perform size and shape discrimination tasks at occupational training and job placements • Student works at meeting size and shape discrimination requirements on job site with supervisor • Student practices working to meet size and shape discrimination requirements with coworker • Student seeks assistance from adult/peer
2. Demonstrate color discrimination	• Student pairs discuss how to perform color discrimination tasks at occupational training and job placements • Student role plays performing in situations requiring color discrimination • Student discusses what actions to take to perform color discrimination tasks at occupational training and job placements • Student practices working to perform color discrimination tasks at occupational training and job placements • Student seeks assistance from teacher	• Student practices performing color discrimination tasks at occupational training and job placements • Student lists appropriate actions to take to perform color discrimination tasks at occupational training and job placements • Student works at meeting color discrimination requirements on job site with supervisor • Student practices working to meet color discrimination requirements with coworker • Student seeks assistance from adult/peer
3. Demonstrate auditory discrimination	• Student pairs discuss how to perform auditory discrimination tasks at occupational training and job placements • Student role plays performing in situations requiring auditory discrimination • Student discusses what actions to take to perform auditory discrimination tasks at occupational training and job placements • Student practices working to perform auditory discrimination tasks at occupational training and job placements • Student seeks assistance from teacher	• Student practices performing auditory discrimination tasks at occupational training and job placements • Student lists appropriate actions to take to perform auditory discrimination tasks at occupational training and job placements • Student works at meeting auditory discrimination requirements on job site with supervisor • Student practices working to meet auditory discrimination requirements with coworker • Student seeks assistance from adult/peer
4. Demonstrate adequate sensory discrimination in occupational training and job placements	• Student pairs discuss how to perform sensory discrimination tasks at occupational training and job placements • Student role plays performing in situations requiring sensory discrimination • Student demonstrates what actions to take to perform sensory discrimination tasks at occupational training and job placements	• Student practices performing sensory discrimination tasks at occupational training and job placements • Student lists appropriate actions to take to perform sensory discrimination tasks at occupational training and job placements • Student works at meeting sensory discrimination requirements on job site with supervisor

	Training Activities	Home-/Community-Based Training Activities
	• Student practices working to perform sensory discrimination tasks at occupational training and job placements • Student seeks assistance from teacher	• Student practices working to meet sensory discrimination requirements with coworker • Student seeks assistance from adult/peer
5. Request assistance in developing size, shape, color, auditory, and sensory discrimination in occupational training and job placements	• HRM discusses sources for assistance in developing size, shape, color, auditory, and sensory discrimination • Student identifies sources for help in developing size, shape, color, auditory, and sensory discrimination to teacher • Student role plays seeking help to improve size, shape, color, auditory, and sensory discrimination • Student states how to seek help in improving size, shape, color, auditory, and sensory discrimination • Student requests help for making improvements in size, shape, color, auditory, and sensory discrimination • Student seeks assistance from teacher	• HRM discusses sources for assistance in developing size, shape, color, auditory, and sensory discrimination • Student demonstrates an understanding of seeking help to improve size, shape, color, auditory, and sensory discrimination • Student requests assistance in developing size, shape, color, auditory, and sensory discrimination • Student demonstrates an understanding of seeking help in developing size, shape, color, auditory, and sensory discrimination • Student seeks assistance from personnel officer for developing size, shape, color, auditory, and sensory discrimination • Student seeks assistance from adult/peer

Domain: Occupational Guidance and Preparation
Competency 19: Matching Physical/Manual Skills to Occupational Training and Employment
Subcompetency 75: Demonstrate Stamina and Endurance

Objectives	Training Activities	Home-/Community-Based Training Activities
1. Identify need for stamina and endurance in occupational training programs and job placements	• HRM discusses reasons for good stamina and endurance in occupational training and job placements • Student role plays scenarios depicting reasons for good stamina and endurance at occupational training and job placements • Student develops list of reasons why good stamina and endurance are important at occupational training and job placements • Student develops poster/chart listing reasons for having good stamina and endurance at occupational training and job placements • Student seeks assistance from teacher	• Student speaks with HRM about reasons for good stamina and endurance in occupational training and job placements • Student provides, with adult/peer, five reasons for good stamina and endurance at occupational training and job placements • Student discusses with HRM reasons why it is important to have good stamina and endurance at occupational training and job placements • Student discusses with adult/peer reasons for good stamina and endurance at occupational training and job placements • Student seeks assistance from adult/peer
2. Identify jobs in which stamina and endurance are critical	• Student develops a list of jobs requiring good stamina and endurance • Guest speaker discusses the many jobs requiring good stamina and endurance • Student develops poster identifying 20 jobs requiring good stamina and endurance • Student seeks assistance from teacher	• Student visits jobs that require good stamina and endurance • Student visits several job sites and identifies the jobs that require good stamina and endurance • Student discusses with adult/peer several jobs that require good stamina and endurance • Student seeks assistance from adult/peer

OCCUPATIONAL GUIDANCE AND PREPARATION

3. Work at demonstrating satisfactory stamina and endurance in occupational training programs and job placements

- Student practices working to build up stamina and endurance in simulated occupational settings
- Student pairs demonstrate how to perform tasks requiring good stamina and endurance at occupational training and job placements
- Student role plays situations requiring good stamina and endurance
- Student demonstrates what actions to take to perform tasks requiring good stamina and endurance at occupational training and job placements
- Student practices working to perform tasks requiring good stamina and endurance at occupational training and job placements
- Student seeks assistance from teacher

- Student practices working to build up stamina and endurance in occupational training programs and job placements
- Student practices performing tasks requiring good stamina and endurance at occupational training and job placements
- Student lists appropriate actions to take to to perform tasks requiring good stamina and endurance at occupational training and job placements
- Student works at meeting good stamina and endurance requirements on job site with supervisor
- Student practices working to meet good stamina and endurance requirements with coworker
- Student seeks assistance from adult/peer

4. Request assistance in developing satisfactory stamina and endurance in occupational training and job placements

- HRM discusses sources for assistance in developing good stamina and endurance
- Student identifies sources for help in developing good stamina and endurance to teacher
- Student role plays seeking help to improve stamina and endurance
- Student states how to seek help in improving stamina and endurance
- Student requests help for making improvements in stamina and endurance
- Student seeks assistance from teacher

- HRM discusses sources for assistance in developing good stamina and endurance
- Student demonstrates an understanding of seeking help to improve stamina and endurance
- Student requests assistance in developing good stamina and endurance
- Student demonstrates an understanding of seeking help in developing good stamina and endurance
- Student seeks assistance from personnel officer for developing good stamina and endurance
- Student seeks assistance from adult/peer

Domain: Occupational Guidance and Preparation
Competency 20: Training for Occupational Choices
There are no specific subcompetencies, since they depend on the specific occupational choice being taught.

OCCUPATIONAL GUIDANCE
AND PREPARATION

3. Assessment and Instructional Planning Strategies

INTRODUCTION

Assessment of the 20 major competencies and 75 subcompetencies is a critical process in the implementation of the LCCE Modified Curriculum. It not only provides information regarding what competencies and subcompetencies have been acquired, but also determines where to begin instruction and whether or not competence was achieved after instruction/training. The field-tested competencies and subcompetencies were established to address the transitional outcomes of students with moderate disabilities. The related behavioral objectives represent tasks which the student should be able to perform to demonstrate acquisition and mastery of the subcompetencies that ultimately lead to mastery of the competency. These objectives provide a comprehensive set of transitional goals and outcomes for this population.

In a competency-based curriculum, mastery and acquisition can best be measured by comparing students to themselves, as opposed to comparing them to other students. This is especially important in meeting the individual needs of students with moderate disabilities. The major assessment instrument suggested for use in preparing to implement the LCCE Modified Curriculum is the Competency Rating Scale-Modified (CRS-M). The CRS-M was developed as a systematic approach to organizing and standardizing the assessment of students in the LCCE Modified Curriculum program. The CRS-M Manual, presented in Appendix A, provides a detailed explanation of the CRS-M instrument and the procedures for administering it. The Manual may be copied for use in home and community settings.

The CRS-M is a rating scale built around the 20 competencies and 75 subcompetencies of the curriculum. The 75 subcompetencies serve as the actual assessment rating items. The Manual presents the criteria (objectives) for judging student mastery of a subcompetency. These criteria are to be rated by at least three individuals who are knowledgeable about the student's performance on the subcompetencies. The use of the specific objectives and rating values is intended to enhance the reliability and validity of the ratings.

Descriptions of who should do the rating, criteria for rating, when rating should be done, a rating key defining numerical rating values, and CRS-M Record Forms for recording and summarizing ratings as well as recording demographic data are all included in the CRS-M Manual. CRS-M users are encouraged to perform an initial rating to be followed by a readministration at least every 2 years. The rater can assign a rating of the degree of mastery (0 = Not Competent, 1 = Partially Competent, and 2 = Competent) for each subcompetency based on the objective's criteria. Ratings are recorded and summarized on the appropriate CRS-M Record Forms (see Appendix B). Results of CRS-M ratings can be used to develop individualized transitional goals and objectives and to measure students' transitional outcomes success.

This technique for assessing mastery of the curriculum is unique in that it offers a measure of LCCE Modified Curriculum transition competency outcomes. Thus, we believe that educators, parents, and community support personnel will find it useful in their efforts to provide transitional programming to individuals with moderate disabilities.

INDIVIDUALIZED EDUCATION PROGRAM (IEP)

The Education for All Handicapped Children Act of 1975 (P.L. 94-142) mandated the establishment of an IEP for every student with a disability. In 1990, P.L. 101-476 gave this Act a new title, The Individuals with Disabilities Education Act (IDEA). One of the most important provisions was a mandate that every eligible student have transition services incorporated into his or her IEP no later than age 14 or as early as the initial IEP. It may be appropriate to include a statement of the interagency responsibilities or linkages in the IEP before the student leaves the school setting. In an attempt to assist educators in fulfilling this requirement, a suggested IEP structure and form for including transition services is presented in this chapter. This form in Appendix C serves as an illustration of how the LCCE approach can be integrated into an IEP or individual transition program (ITP) format. State and local education agencies will have their own forms and requirements. The LCCE IEP form consists of the following sections:

Section I: Present Level of Educational Performance
Section II: Annual Goals
Section III: Specific Educational Services Needed
Section IV: Short-Term Individual Objectives
Section V: Dates and Lengths of Times of Specific Educational Services
Section VI: Extent of Participation in Regular Program
Section VII: Placement Justification
Section VIII: Individuals Responsible for Implementation
Section IX: Evaluation Criteria, Procedures, and Schedule
Section X: Day, Location, and Time of Next IEP Conference

The CRS-M can be used in both the development and evaluation of the functional skills/transition component of the IEP. For example, the present level of educational performance in Section I can be partly determined by the CRS-M results. The annual functional skills/transition goals for Section II can be chosen from the 20 competencies.

The specific educational services in Section III can be selected from the 75 subcompetencies as well as from other sources. The short-term objectives in Section IV can also be selected from the 75 subcompetencies. The CRS-M can be used to evaluate the degree of mastery of these short-term objectives, since the CRS-M items are identical to the subcompetencies. Section IX can be completed using CRS-M behavioral criteria/objectives. The CRS-M is an appropriate evaluation measure. Thus, an IEP with functional skills and transition components can be constructed from the LCCE Modified Curriculum competencies and subcompetencies from the information provided on the CRS-M.

The assessment and instructional planning processes are critical for determining the student's needs in preparing to make the transition from school to work and community living. The LCCE Modified Curriculum's CRS-M and IEP are valuable tools for assisting students with moderate disabilities in achieving a successful transition outcome.

Appendix A
Competency Rating Scale-Modified (CRS-M) for Life Centered Career Education (LCCE) Modified Curriculum for Individuals with Moderate Disabilities

INTRODUCTION

The Life Centered Career Education (LCCE) curriculum is a competency-based approach. There are 22 competencies in the original LCCE Curriculum (Brolin, 1974) and 20 competencies in the LCCE Modified Curriculum (Loyd & Brolin, 1997) that have been identified as necessary for achieving successful adult adjustment for students with mild or moderate disabilities. These competencies have been broken down further into subcompetencies and their objectives. The Competency Rating Scale-Modified (CRS-M) provides users with a systematic means of assessing student mastery of the subcompetencies. This manual furnishes the criteria/objectives for rating students' performance and mastery of each of the 75 subcompetencies making up the LCCE Modified Curriculum for Individuals with Moderate Disabilities.

The user completes the CRS-M by judging the student's mastery of the subcompetencies using the performance criteria/objectives presented in Section III of this manual. Since the CRS-M requires judgments regarding student per-

formance and behavior, it is necessary that all raters employ the same criteria when making judgment decisions. This is critical if the user intends to make comparisons of the student's performance or behavior over time.

This manual is divided into four sections. Section I describes the rating key and how to rate student performance and behavior. Section II explains the use of the CRS-M Form. Section III presents explanations and behavioral criteria/objectives for the subcompetencies. Section IV describes the interpretation of CRS-M results.

The task of evaluating the performance of students with moderate disabilities in any functional academic area is a difficult one. This task becomes increasingly more difficult for educators dealing with the transitional education of these students.

SECTION I—RATING STUDENT PERFORMANCE

The Rating Key

The CRS-M provides three alternative ratings for student performance on each subcompetency. There are three sources from which the user can draw information to establish the rating for a given subcompetency. The most valid evaluation is the rater's personal observation of the student's performance and behavior. Ratings from other personnel who have observed the student's performance and behavior are less valid, but acceptable. Finally, the student's personal assessment of her or his performance and behavior is the least valid, but it may be of some assistance in identifying the student's personal perceptions of abilities.

When sufficient information exists to rate a subcompetency, one of the following ratings should be selected:

0 = *Not Competent.* The student is unable to perform any of the behavioral criteria/objectives for the subcompetency. This rating should be used for students who, in the judgment of the rater, cannot be expected to perform this subcompetency satisfactorily and who would need support in normalized/integrated environments. This student needs additional training, or, if such training is not available, will need the support of some advocate or agency personnel to partially or fully participate in activities requiring the subcompetency skills.

1 = *Partially Competent.* The student is able to perform at least one but not all of the behavioral criteria/objectives for the subcompetency. This rating should be used for students who, in the judgment of the rater, can be expected to perform this subcompetency partially or fully in integrated or normalized environments with the support of an advocate or agency personnel.

2 = *Competent.* The student is able to perform all of the behavioral criteria/objectives for the subcompetency. This rating should be used when the rater is confident that the student can satisfactorily perform this subcompetency in integrated or normalized environments.

NR = *Not Rated.* The rater feels that she or he is unable to rate the student's performance at this time. This may be due to a lack of time to collect sufficient information about the student's performance or behavior or lack of information to validate a rating.

If the student leaves formal education without a competent rating (2) for a subcompetency, then he or she should seek additional training (advocates or community agencies) and/or request necessary support. A unique feature in this curriculum is that for each of the subcompetencies students are taught to seek assistance and support when needed. This student empowerment strategy has been embedded into the curriculum to prepare the student to request supports necessary for integration into normalized environments.

The Rater

Optimally, the same individual should rate a student's performance and behavior for all of the subcompetencies in a particular domain. However, it is also recommended that others who are knowledgeable about the student's performance and behavior rate the student. These can include parents, previous teachers/trainers, community agency personnel, and/or siblings. It may be necessary to have several raters complete the rating scale. If this occurs, then it is recommended that each rater complete at least one of the three LCCE domains. Each completed rating scale should be discussed with the student's support team and used to help complete the student's individualized education program (IEP), or individualized work rehabilitation plan (IWRP), or individualized habilitation plan (IHP).

Rating Intervals

Space is provided on Section II of the CRS-M Record Form (see Appendix B) for seven ratings. It is suggested that the CRS-M be administered prior to the first IEP conference and each 2 years thereafter. These forms can be duplicated and ratings completed as often as necessary.

SECTION II—USING THE CRS-M RECORD FORM

The CRS-M Record Form is separated into three sections corresponding to the three functional curriculum domains: Daily Living Skills, Personal-Social Skills, and Occupational Guidance and Preparation. Although it is best to complete the CRS-M all at one time, each domain can be administered independently. As noted in Section I of this manual, it is desirable that one individual rate all subcompetencies in a particular domain. The blank CRS-M Record Form presented in Appendix B may be used as a master for duplication.

Identifying Information

The CRS-M Record Form provides space to record the student's name, date of birth, and sex. Space is also provided for the name and address of the student's school.

Directions

The directions for the CRS-M Record Form indicate that the user should choose one of the four possible ratings for each subcompetency. The numerical ratings should be recorded in the space to the right of the subcompetency. The NR rating should be assigned to items that are not rated. The subcompetencies are listed on the left side of the CRS-M Record Form and are grouped under the competencies. Space is provided at the head of each rating column to record the rater's name(s), the student's grade level, and the date(s) of the rating period. If the ratings are completed in a single day, only that date need be recorded. However, if the ratings require more than 1 day, the user should record both the beginning and ending dates. It is recommended that ratings be completed as quickly as possible (i.e., 1 day to 1 week).

Note that Competency 20 in the Occupational Guidance and Preparation domain has no subcompetencies. Space is provided following Competency 20 to list specific occupational skill training the student is receiving. The rater should rate this training in the same manner as the other subcompetencies by treating the skill training as a subcompetency.

Space is also provided following the list of subcompetencies for the total possible score if a student were assigned the highest rating for each subcompetency in a domain. This value is determined by omitting Competency 20 from the calculations. The total possible score can be calculated by counting the number of rated items (N) and multiplying by the highest possible rating (2). Thus, total possible score (TPS) = N $\times$ 2. To the right of the total possible score, space is provided to record the student's total actual score (TAS), which is the sum of the ratings for all rated items. Space is provided below the TAS to record the average score per item (AS). The AS is calculated by dividing the TAS by N; thus, AS = TAS $\div$ N. Space is provided at the end of the Occupational Guidance and Preparation section for a cumulative total possible score, a cumulative total actual score, and a cumulative average score. The cumulative TPS can be calculated by adding the TPSs for the three domains. *Note:* The TPS and cumulative TPS must be calculated for *each* administration since the number of rated items may vary with each administration. The cumulative TAS can be calculated by the TASs from the three domains. The cumulative AS can be calculated by adding the ASs from the three domains and dividing by three. Thus, the user can evaluate performance and behavior for each domain as well as the three domains combined. There is space provided for comments at the end of each record form.

SECTION III—BEHAVIORAL CRITERIA/ OBJECTIVES FOR RATING SUBCOMPETENCIES

A list of the 75 subcompetencies grouped into the three functional curriculum domains follows. Each subcompetency is described conceptually and further defined by behavioral criteria/objectives. As discussed in Section I, the rater should compare student performance to the behavioral criteria/objectives for each subcompetency to determine the degree of mastery. The ratings from the rating key can then be assigned to each subcompetency (item) based on the number of criteria/objectives that the student is able to perform for each subcompetency.

DAILY LIVING SKILLS

1. Managing Money

1. *Count Money*
   1. Identify coins
   2. Count sums of up to five coins from stacks of pennies, nickels, dimes, quarters, and half dollars
   3. Identify bills up to $20
   4. Count currency with sums less than $20
2. *Make Purchases*
   1. Select appropriate item
   2. Recognize and request assistance
   3. Locate cashier
   4. Calculate and give appropriate purchase amount
   5. Receive purchase and change
3. *Use Vending Machines*
   1. Select appropriate coins
   2. Operate vending machines
   3. Receive vending machine purchase and change
   4. Recognize and request assistance as needed
4. *Budget Money*
   1. Identify weekly personal income
   2. Identify weekly and/or monthly expenses
   3. Calculate daily/weekly/monthly expenses to personal income
   4. Compare expenses to date with remaining personal income
5. *Perform Banking Skills*
   1. Open checking account
   2. Open savings account
   3. Write checks and record transactions
   4. Make deposits and record transactions
   5. Request banking assistance
   6. Use check cashing cards/services

2. Selecting and Maintaining Living Environments

6. *Select Appropriate Community Living Environments*
   1. Identify available living environments
   2. Choose appropriate living environments
   3. Identify procedures for renting and connecting utilities
7. *Maintain Living Environment*
   1. Identify routine cleaning tasks
   2. Plan daily/weekly cleaning routine
   3. Identify and use common household cleaning products
   4. Identify and demonstrate safe use of household cleaning products
   5. Perform daily/weekly cleaning routine
   6. Identify when and where to obtain common household cleaning products
8. *Use Basic Appliances and Tools*
   1. Identify common household appliances and tools and their uses

    2. Demonstrate appropriate use of common household appliances and tools

    3. Identify safety procedures when using household appliances and tools

    4. Request appropriate assistance for household repair tasks

9. *Set Up Personal Living Space*
    1. Identify and select personal living space
    2. Identify and select personal living furnishings
    3. Arrange personal living space

3. Caring for Personal Health

10. *Perform Appropriate Grooming and Hygiene*
    1. Identify grooming products and where to obtain them
    2. Identify and practice body care skills
    3. Identify and practice oral/dental hygiene skills
    4. Identify and practice hair care skills
    5. Identify and practice toileting skills

11. *Dress Appropriately*
    1. Select clothing for different weather conditions
    2. Select clothing for different activities
    3. Select and coordinate well-fitting clothing
    4. Maintain neat appearance

12. *Maintain Physical Fitness*
    1. Identify physical exercises/activities
    2. Practice physical exercises/activities daily

13. *Recognize and Seek Help for Illness*
    1. Identify signs/symptoms of common illnesses/diseases
    2. Contact medical assistance

14. *Practice Basic First Aid*
    1. Perform basic first aid measures
    2. Identify emergency situations
    3. Contact emergency assistance
    4. Follow emergency procedures

15. *Practice Personal Safety*
    1. Identify situations that are dangerous in the home, community, and at work
    2. Identify safety precautions to avoid personal injury in the home, community, and at work
    3. Identify self-protection procedures
    4. Practice precautions when dealing with strangers

4. Developing and Maintaining Appropriate Intimate Relationships

16. *Demonstrate Knowledge of Basic Human Sexuality*
    1. Identify basic male and female sexual differences
    2. Describe the human reproduction process
    3. Discuss personal responsibilities/behaviors

17. *Demonstrate Knowledge of Appropriate Dating Behavior*
    1. Identify the physical needs of dating
    2. Identify the social-emotional needs of dating
    3. State parents'/guardians' position on dating/dating behavior

5. Eating at Home and in the Community

18. *Plan Balanced Meals*
    1. Identify the four basic food groups
    2. Identify appropriate foods eaten at typical daily meals
    3. Plan weekly menu

19. *Purchase Food*
    1. Construct shopping list from weekly word or picture menu
    2. Locate food items on list
    3. Recognize and request assistance as needed
    4. Locate cashier
    5. Calculate and give appropriate purchase amount
    6. Receive purchase and change

20. *Prepare Meals*
    1. Identify food preparation procedures
    2. Identify and demonstrate use of basic kitchen tools and appliances
    3. Select recipe
    4. Collect foods and utensils listed on recipe
    5. Follow simple recipe

21. *Demonstrate Appropriate Eating Habits*
    1. Demonstrate table setting
    2. Demonstrate appropriate serving of food
    3. Demonstrate appropriate eating manners

22. *Demonstrate Meal Clean-Up and Food Storage*
    1. Demonstrate meal clean-up procedures
    2. Identify signs of food spoilage
    3. Demonstrate waste disposal procedures
    4. Sort food into storage groups
    5. Demonstrate appropriate food storage

23. *Demonstrate Appropriate Restaurant Dining*
    1. Identify types of restaurants
    2. Estimate meal costs and bring sufficient money to dine out
    3. Order from wall/printed menus
    4. Demonstrate eating manners
    5. Pay bill and tip appropriately

6. Cleaning and Purchasing Clothing

24. *Wash/Dry Clothes*
    1. Identify types and uses of laundry products
    2. Sort clothing by temperature, load, and colors
    3. Load clothes
    4. Add detergent
    5. Set temperatures and load settings
    6. Start washing machine
    7. Remove clothes at end of washing cycle and hang non-dryable clothes up to dry
    8. Load washed clothes in dryer
    9. Set temperature and time dials
    10. Start dryer
    11. Remove clothes from dryer and hang or fold at end of drying cycle
    12. Store clothes
    13. Perform any upkeep procedures
    14. Perform washing/drying clothes at laundromat

25. *Buy Clothes*
    1. Identify basic clothing needs
    2. Identify size, color, and style of clothing needed
    3. Estimate clothing costs and bring money for clothing needs
    4. Identify appropriate clothing store
    5. Locate appropriate store department
    6. Request assistance from store clerk

7. Select clothing item(s)
8. Check fit of clothing item(s)
9. Locate cashier
10. Calculate and give appropriate purchase amount
11. Receive purchase and change

7. Participate in Leisure/Recreational Activities

26. *Identify Available Community Leisure/Recreational Activities*
    1. Identify types of individual leisure/recreational activities
    2. Identify types of group leisure/recreational activities
    3. Locate equipment and facilities of leisure/recreational activities
27. *Select and Plan Leisure/Recreational Activities*
    1. Identify personal leisure/recreational activities and interests
    2. Identify costs, time, and physical requirements of leisure/recreational activities
    3. Develop weekly schedule of leisure/recreational activities
28. *Participate in Individual and Group Leisure/Recreational Activities*
    1. Identify and obtain necessary equipment
    2. Identify and follow rules of leisure/recreational activities
29. *Select and Participate in Group Travel*
    1. Identify travel interests
    2. Identify travel possibilities
    3. Identify expenses and resources needed for travel
    4. Request assistance in travel planning
    5. Demonstrate appropriate travel behavior

8. Getting Around in the Community

30. *Follow Traffic Rules and Safety Procedures*
    1. Identify common traffic and safety signs and rules
    2. Practice following common traffic and safety signs and rules
31. *Develop and Follow Community Access Routes*
    1. Identify routinely used community locations
    2. Plan and practice following important community routes
    3. Request assistance as needed
32. *Access Available Transportation*
    1. Identify modes of transportation in the community
    2. Identify requirements of each mode of community transportation
    3. Practice using modes of community transportation
    4. Request assistance for using modes of community transportation
    5. Identify and develop strategies for coping with disruption in primary community transportation mode

PERSONAL-SOCIAL SKILLS

9. Acquiring Self-Identity

33. *Demonstrate Knowledge of Personal Interests and Abilities*
    1. Identify and describe personal interests
    2. Identify and describe personal abilities
34. *Demonstrate Appropriate Responses to Emotions*
    1. Identify different emotions
    2. Identify ways to express emotions
    3. Practice appropriate ways to express emotions
    4. Request assistance for coping with emotions
35. *Display Self-Confidence and Self-Worth*
    1. Identify positive aspects of people in general
    2. Identify positive aspects of self
    3. Practice displaying self-confidence and self-worth
36. *Demonstrate Giving and Accepting Praise and Criticism*
    1. Identify critical statements
    2. Identify statements of praise
    3. Identify appropriate/inappropriate responses to criticism
    4. Identify appropriate/inappropriate responses to praise
    5. Respond to accepting criticism
    6. Respond to receiving praise

10. Exhibiting Socially Responsible Behavior

37. *Demonstrate Appropriate Behavior*
    1. Identify appropriate/inappropriate behavior at home
    2. Identify appropriate/inappropriate behavior at work
    3. Identify appropriate/inappropriate behavior at training programs
    4. Identify appropriate/inappropriate behavior in the community
    5. Practice appropriate behavior at home
    6. Practice appropriate behavior at work
    7. Practice appropriate behavior at school/training program
    8. Practice appropriate behavior in the community
38. *Identify Current and Future Personal Roles*
    1. Identify current personal roles
    2. Identify possible future personal roles
    3. Describe how personal roles differ from those of significant others
    4. Describe how personal roles interact with others' roles
39. *Demonstrate Respect for Others' Rights and Property*
    1. Identify personal property and rights of others
    2. Identify reasons for respecting personal property and rights of others
    3. Practice respecting others' personal property and rights
    4. Identify actions for borrowing items
    5. Identify actions when others' personal property has been damaged
    6. Identify actions when others' personal rights have been violated
40. *Demonstrate Respect for Authority*
    1. Identify authority figures
    2. Identify roles of authority figures
    3. Identify consequences of not respecting authority
    4. Practice respecting authority
41. *Demonstrate Ability to Follow Directions/Instructions*
    1. Identify importance of following authority directions/instructions
    2. Identify actions of not following authority directions/instructions
    3. Practice following authority directions/instructions
42. *Demonstrate Appropriate Citizen Rights and Responsibilities*
    1. Identify community services available to citizens
    2. Locate community services available to citizens

 3. Identify major rights of citizens
 4. Identify major responsibilities of citizens
 5. Identify citizens' duties to governments
 6. Practice being a good citizen

43. *Identify How Personal Behavior Affects Others*
 1. Identify how personal behavior can affect others
 2. Identify cues others provide when personal behavior is inappropriate
 3. Describe ways to change inappropriate behavior

11. Developing and Maintaining Appropriate Social Relationships

44. *Develop Friendships*
 1. Identify why friendship is important
 2. Identify characteristics of friendship
 3. Describe how to select a friend
 4. Practice developing friends
45. *Maintain Friendships*
 1. Identify ways to keep and lose friends
 2. Identify how to select a date
 3. Identify procedures for dating
 4. Identify appropriate responses to intimacy with close friends
 5. Practice maintaining friendships

12. Exhibiting Independent Behavior

46. *Set and Reach Personal Goals*
 1. Identify the importance of setting personal goals
 2. Identify how to set goals
 3. Identify reasons to reach goals
 4. Identify how to modify/revise goals
 5. Practice setting and meeting goals
47. *Demonstrate Self-Organization*
 1. Identify routine daily activities
 2. Develop plan of daily activities
 3. Identify areas of responsibility in personal life
 4. Identify importance of organizing personal activities
 5. Practice daily self-organization
 6. Request assistance with self-organization.
48. *Demonstrate Self-Determination*
 1. Identify importance of practicing self-determination
 2. Practice self-determination
 3. Request assistance with self-determination

13. Making Informed Decisions

49. *Identify Problems/Conflicts*
 1. Identify personal problems/conflicts
 2. Identify why personal problems/conflicts exist
 3. Request assistance in identifying personal problems/conflicts
50. *Use Appropriate Resources to Assist in Problem Solving*
 1. Identify situations in which individuals need advice
 2. Identify available sources for providing assistance in resolving personal problems/conflicts
 3. Identify outcomes of seeking help in resolving personal problems/conflicts

 4. Seek appropriate sources in helping to resolve personal problems/conflicts
51. *Develop and Select Best Solution to Problems/Conflicts*
 1. Identify solutions to personal problems/conflicts
 2. Select best solutions developed to personal problems/conflicts
 3. Seek assistance in helping to develop and select best solutions to personal problems/conflicts
 4. Practice developing and selecting best solutions to personal problems/conflicts
52. *Demonstrate Decision Making*
 1. Identify importance of making decisions
 2. Identify steps in making informed decisions
 3. Seek help in making decisions

14. Communicating with Others

53. *Demonstrate Listening and Responding Skills*
 1. Identify the importance of listening and responding
 2. Identify appropriate listening techniques
 3. Identify appropriate responding techniques
 4. Practice attentive listening and responding
54. *Demonstrate Effective Communication*
 1. Identify modes of communication
 2. Identify appropriate speaking methods
 3. Identify inappropriate speaking methods
 4. Identify methods of expressing needs and feelings
 5. Identify appropriate techniques of communicating on the telephone
 6. Identify nonverbal cues and communication skills
 7. Practice effective communication
55. *Communicate in Emergency Situations*
 1. Identify signs of an emergency situation
 2. Identify appropriate authorities to contact in different emergency situations
 3. Practice communicating in emergency situations

OCCUPATIONAL GUIDANCE AND PREPARATION

15. Exploring and Locating Occupational Training and Job Placement Opportunities

56. *Identify Rewards of Working*
 1. Identify the importance of working
 2. Discuss the rewards for working
 3. Identify the reasons some jobs pay more than others
 4. Identify personal needs that are met through work
 5. Identify how work is part of one's personal identity
 6. Identify ways workers contribute to society
 7. Identify ways society rewards different types of jobs
57. *Locate Available Occupational Training and Job Placement Possibilities*
 1. Identify sources for locating occupational training and job placement information
 2. Discuss different types of occupational training possibilities
 3. Identify general job placement possibilities
 4. Identify general training possibilities

5. Practice locating available occupational training possibilities

6. Request assistance for locating occupational training possibilities

16. Making Occupational Training and Job Placement Choices

58. *Demonstrate Knowledge of Occupational Interests*
    1. Identify occupational interests
    2. Discuss types of jobs matching personal occupational interests
    3. Request assistance regarding matching jobs with personal occupational interests

59. *Demonstrate Knowledge of Occupational Strengths and Weaknesses*
    1. Identify occupational strengths and weaknesses
    2. Discuss jobs matching personal occupational strengths
    3. Request assistance regarding matching jobs with personal occupational strengths

60. *Identify Possible and Available Jobs Matching Interests and Strengths*
    1. Identify jobs of interest
    2. State jobs of interest that match personal occupational strengths and weaknesses
    3. Discuss job-related requirements of jobs matching personal occupational interests

61. *Plan and Make Realistic Occupational Training and Job Placement Decisions*
    1. Identify occupational training and job placement options
    2. Develop plan to meet identified occupational training and job placement options
    3. Request assistance to help plan and make realistic occupational training and job placement choices

62. *Develop Training Plan for Occupational Choice*
    1. Identify steps in developing occupational choice training plan
    2. Develop occupational choice training plan

17. Applying for and Maintaining Occupational Training and Job Placements

63. *Apply for Occupational Training and Job Placements*
    1. Identify steps in applying for occupational training and job placements
    2. Collect and develop personal data card for completing application forms
    3. Complete applications for occupational training and job placements
    4. Request assistance in applying for occupational training and/or job placements

64. *Interview for Occupational Training and Job Placements*
    1. Identify appropriate interview skills for occupational training and job placements
    2. Practice mock interviews for occupational training and job placements
    3. Practice interviews for occupational training and job placements

4. Request help in preparing and interviewing for occupational training and job placements

65. *Make Adjustments to Changes in Employment Status*
    1. Identify potential problems encountered in occupational training and job placements
    2. Identify potential solutions to problems encountered in occupational training and job placements
    3. Identify factors that determine successful work adjustment
    4. Identify factors that determine unsuccessful work adjustment
    5. Identify reasons for occupational training or employment changes or termination
    6. Identify factors relating to being promoted in jobs
    7. Request assistance in making changes in employment status

18. Developing and Maintaining Appropriate Work Skills and Behavior

66. *Perform Work Directions and Meet Requirements*
    1. Identify the importance of following directions and meeting requirements
    2. Perform a series of tasks in response to verbal instructions

67. *Maintain Good Attendance and Punctuality*
    1. Identify reasons for good attendance and punctuality
    2. Identify actions to take for tardiness or absence from work

68. *Respond Appropriately to Supervision*
    1. Identify appropriate behavior when being supervised
    2. Exhibit appropriate response to supervision

69. *Demonstrate Job Safety*
    1. Identify the importance of job safety
    2. Identify potential job hazards
    3. Identify safety measures in job choices
    4. Exhibit job safety

70. *Work Cooperatively with Others*
    1. Identify reasons for working with others
    2. Practice working cooperatively with others

71. *Meet Work Quality and Quantity Standards*
    1. Identify reasons for work quality standards
    2. Identify reasons for work quantity standards
    3. Identify consequences of not meeting work quality and quantity standards
    4. Practice meeting work quality and quantity standards

19. Matching Physical/Manual Skills to Occupational Training and Employment

72. *Demonstrate Fine Motor Dexterity in Occupational Training and Job Placements*
    1. Identify need for good fine motor dexterity in occupational training and employment
    2. Identify jobs in which fine motor dexterity is critical
    3. Demonstrate fine motor dexterity in occupational training programs and/or at job sites
    4. Request assistance in developing fine motor dexterity in occupational training and job placements

73. *Demonstrate Gross Motor Dexterity in Occupational Training and Job Placements*
    1. Identify need for gross motor dexterity in occupational training and employment
    2. Identify jobs in which gross motor dexterity is critical
    3. Demonstrate gross motor dexterity in occupational training programs and/or at job sites
    4. Request assistance in developing gross motor dexterity in occupational training and job placements
74. *Demonstrate Sensory Discrimination in Occupational Training and Job Placements*
    1. Demonstrate size and shape discrimination
    2. Demonstrate color discrimination
    3. Demonstrate auditory discrimination
    4. Demonstrate adequate sensory discrimination in occupational training and job placements
    5. Request assistance in developing size, shape, color, auditory, and sensory discrimination in occupational training and job placements
75. *Demonstrate Stamina and Endurance*
    1. Identify need for stamina and endurance in occupational training programs and job placements
    2. Identify jobs in which stamina and endurance are critical
    3. Work at demonstrating satisfactory stamina and endurance in occupational training programs and job placements
    4. Request assistance in developing satisfactory stamina and endurance in occupational training and job placements

20. Training for Occupational Choices

There are no specific subcompetencies since they depend on the skill being taught.

SECTION IV—INTERPRETATION

Each user will have to decide whether a complete mastery of a specified percentage of subcompetencies is preferable to a partial mastery of all of the subcompetencies. At this time, the suggested method of interpretation involves the user's identification of student strengths and weaknesses. Such identification should prove useful for developing individualized education programs (IEPs) as well as evaluating IEP outcomes. Since the CRS-M items are actually the subcompetencies of the LCCE Modified Curriculum, low-rated items can be used to establish short-term objectives for individualized functional planning. Readministration of the CRS-M can then be used to evaluate the effectiveness of such planning by comparing pre- and postintervention ratings.

The CRS-M user can review student performance and behavior for any given rating period to determine deficient areas. Such a determination can assist both in general curriculum planning and in individualized functional planning.

If a large percentage of students are deficient in particular areas (subcompetencies, competencies, or domains), emphasis on these areas could be incorporated into functional planning and training. Individual weaknesses can be addressed through revised IEPs. Note that the rating key allows only three numerical ratings. The operational definition of the 1 rating ("at least one, but not all") makes student progress on a subcompetency possible without a change in numerical rating. A student might require several years to progress from a rating of 1 on an individual subcompetency to a rating of 2. Therefore, in the IEP evaluation, the user should look for short-term gains in the larger categories (competencies or domains). This system will reflect short-term gains when used in this manner.

The CRS-M user can review student performance and behavior over several rating periods to determine progress as well as establish realistic expectancies for typical student growth and development. This interpretation provides not only suggestions for immediate functional curriculum planning on a general and individual basis, but also suggestions for long-range functional curriculum sequencing. This type of data should prove particularly useful after systematic analysis, since there is little information available to predict typical developmental stages in the career development of students with mild or moderate disabilities.

Although the subcompetencies, competencies, and domains identified here are felt to be generally comprehensive, there is no evidence at present that these divisions and their sequencing correlate strongly with student ability to master these objectives at any particular age or developmental stage. Thus, the CRS-M user has an opportunity to either formally or informally establish expectancies and sequencing in each particular setting.

In summary, CRS-M results can be employed to:

- Determine students' strengths and weaknesses.
- Develop and review IEPs.
- Plan and develop a functional/transitional curriculum.
- Monitor student or group progress.

The CRS-M is an integral part of the assessment process for the LCCE-Modified Curriculum program. The CRS-M results should be included in the student's transition portfolio and should accompany the student when seeking support from other adult service providers or seeking employment. This instrument should be a valuable tool for all students with moderate disabilities in K through 12+ transition planning.

Appendix B
Competency Rating Scale (CRS) Master Forms for the Life Centered Career Education (LCCE) Modified Curriculum for Individuals with Moderate Disabilities

The forms on the following pages are designed to be reproduced for use with the Life Centered Career Education (LCCE) Modified Curriculum. The following forms are given:

- Competency Rating Scale-Modified
    Daily Living Skills
    Personal-Social Skills
    Occupational Guidance and Preparation

LIFE CENTERED CAREER EDUCATION
Competency Rating Scale-Modified
Record Form
DAILY LIVING SKILLS

Student Name _____ Date of Birth _____ Sex _____

School _____City _____ State _____

Directions: Please rate the student according to his/her mastery of *each* item using the rating key below. Indicate the ratings in the column below the date for the rating period. Use the NR rating for items which cannot be rated. For subcompetencies rated 0 or 1 at the time of the final rating, place a check (✔) in the appropriate space in the *yes/no* column to indicate his/her ability to perform the subcompetency with assistance from the community. Please refer to the CRS manual for explanation of the rating key, description of the behavioral criteria for each subcompetency, and explanation of the *yes/no* column.

Rating Key: 0 = Not Competent   1 = Partially Competent   2 = Competent   NR = Not Related

To what extent has the student mastered the following subcompetencies?

Subcompetencies	Rater(s)									
	Grade Level									
	Date(s)									
DAILY LIVING SKILLS DOMAIN									Yes	No
1. Managing Money										
1. Count Money	—	—	—	—	—	—	—	—	—	
2. Make Purchases	—	—	—	—	—	—	—	—	—	
3. Use Vending Machines	—	—	—	—	—	—	—	—	—	
4. Budget Money	—	—	—	—	—	—	—	—	—	
5. Perform Banking Skills	—	—	—	—	—	—	—	—	—	
2. Selecting and Maintaining Living Environments										
6. Select Appropriate Community Living Environments	—	—	—	—	—	—	—	—	—	
7. Maintain Living Environment	—	—	—	—	—	—	—	—	—	
8. Use Basic Appliances and Tools	—	—	—	—	—	—	—	—	—	
9. Set Up Personal Living Space	—	—	—	—	—	—	—	—	—	
3. Caring for Personal Health										
10. Perform Appropriate Grooming and Hygiene	—	—	—	—	—	—	—	—	—	—
11. Dress Appropriately	—	—	—	—	—	—	—	—	—	—
12. Maintain Physical Fitness	—	—	—	—	—	—	—	—	—	—
13. Recognize and Seek Help for Illness	—	—	—	—	—	—	—	—	—	—
14. Practice Basic First Aid	—	—	—	—	—	—	—	—	—	—
15. Practice Personal Safety	—	—	—	—	—	—	—	—	—	—

Subcompetencies	Rater(s)									
	Grade Level									
	Date(s)									
4. Developing and Maintaining Appropriate Intimate Relationships									Yes	No
16. Demonstrate Knowledge of Basic Human Sexuality	—	—	—	—	—	—	—	—	—	—
17. Demonstrate Knowledge of Appropriate Dating Behavior	—	—	—	—	—	—	—	—	—	—
5. Eating at Home and in the Community										
18. Plan Balanced Meals	—	—	—	—	—	—	—	—	—	—
19. Purchase Food	—	—	—	—	—	—	—	—	—	—
20. Prepare Meals	—	—	—	—	—	—	—	—	—	—
21. Demonstrate Appropriate Eating Habits	—	—	—	—	—	—	—	—	—	—
22. Demonstrate Meal Clean-Up and Food Storage	—	—	—	—	—	—	—	—	—	—
23. Demonstrate Appropriate Restaurant Dining	—	—	—	—	—	—	—	—	—	—
6. Cleaning and Purchasing Clothing										
24. Wash/Dry Clothes	—	—	—	—	—	—	—	—	—	—
25. Buy Clothes	—	—	—	—	—	—	—	—	—	—
7. Participate in Leisure/Recreational Activities										
26. Identify Available Community Leisure/Recreational Activities	—	—	—	—	—	—	—	—	—	—
27. Select and Plan Leisure/Recreational Activities	—	—	—	—	—	—	—	—	—	—
28. Participate in Individual and Group Leisure/ Recreational Activities	—	—	—	—	—	—	—	—	—	—
29. Select and Participate in Group Travel	—	—	—	—	—	—	—	—	—	—
8. Getting Around in the Community										
30. Follow Traffic Rules and Safety Procedures	—	—	—	—	—	—	—	—	—	—
31. Develop and Follow Community Access Routes	—	—	—	—	—	—	—	—	—	—
32. Access Available Transportation	—	—	—	—	—	—	—	—	—	—

Total Possible Score
(TPS) = N 3 2 _____

Total Actual Score
(TAS) — — — — — — —

Average Score
(AS) = TAS/N — — — — — — —

Comments: _____
_____

Use asterisk to denote skill areas of instruction noted in the student's IEP for the year.
Refer to the CRS manual for calculation and interpretation.

LIFE CENTERED CAREER EDUCATION
Competency Rating Scale-Modified
Record Form
PERSONAL-SOCIAL SKILLS

Student Name _____ Date of Birth _____ Sex _____

School _____City _____ State _____

Directions: Please rate the student according to his/her mastery of *each* item using the rating key below. Indicate the ratings in the column below the date for the rating period. Use the NR rating for items which cannot be rated. For subcompetencies rated 0 or 1 at the time of the final rating, place a check (✔) in the appropriate space in the *yes/no* column to indicate his/her ability to perform the subcompetency with assistance from the community. Please refer to the CRS manual for explanation of the rating key, description of the behavioral criteria for each subcompetency, and explanation of the *yes/no* column.

Rating Key: 0 = Not Competent   1 = Partially Competent   2 = Competent   NR = Not Related

To what extent has the student mastered the following subcompetencies?

Subcompetencies	*Rater(s)*									
	Grade Level									
	Date(s)									
PERSONAL-SOCIAL SKILLS DOMAIN									*Yes*	*No*
9. *Acquiring Self-Identity*										
33. Demonstrate Knowledge of Personal Interests and Abilities	—	—	—	—	—	—	—	—	—	—
34. Demonstrate Appropriate Responses to Emotions Criticism	—	—	—	—	—	—	—	—	—	—
35. Display Self-Confidence and Self-Worth	—	—	—	—	—	—	—	—	—	—
36. Demonstrate Giving and Accepting Praise and	—	—	—	—	—	—	—	—	—	—
10. *Exhibiting Socially Responsible Behavior*										
37. Demonstrate Appropriate Behavior	—	—	—	—	—	—	—	—	—	—
38. Identify Current and Future Personal Roles	—	—	—	—	—	—	—	—	—	—
39. Demonstrate Respect for Others' Rights and Property	—	—	—	—	—	—	—	—	—	—
40. Demonstrate Respect for Authority	—	—	—	—	—	—	—	—	—	—
41. Demonstrate Ability to Follow Directions/Instructions	—	—	—	—	—	—	—	—	—	—
42. Demonstrate Appropriate Citizen Rights and Responsibilities	—	—	—	—	—	—	—	—	—	—
43. Identify How Personal Behavior Affects Others	—	—	—	—	—	—	—	—	—	—
11. *Developing and Maintaining Appropriate Social Relationships*										
44. Develop Friendships	—	—	—	—	—	—	—	—	—	—
45. Maintain Friendships	—	—	—	—	—	—	—	—	—	—

Subcompetencies	Rater(s)								
	Grade Level								
	Date(s)								
12. *Exhibiting Independent Behavior*								Yes	No
46. Set and Reach Personal Goals	—	—	—	—	—	—	—	—	—
47. Demonstrate Self-Organization	—	—	—	—	—	—	—	—	—
48. Demonstrate Self-Determination	—	—	—	—	—	—	—	—	—
13. *Making Informed Decisions*									
49. Identify Problems/Conflicts	—	—	—	—	—	—	—	—	—
50. Use Appropriate Resources to Assist in Problem Solving	—	—	—	—	—	—	—	—	—
51. Develop and Select Best Solution to Problems/Conflicts	—	—	—	—	—	—	—	—	—
52. Demonstrate Decision Making	—	—	—	—	—	—	—	—	—
14. *Communicating with Others*									
53. Demonstrate Listening and Responding Skills	—	—	—	—	—	—	—	—	—
54. Demonstrate Effective Communication	—	—	—	—	—	—	—	—	—
55. Communicate in Emergency Situations	—	—	—	—	—	—	—	—	—

Total Possible Score
(TPS) = N 3 2 _____

Total Actual Score
(TAS)   —   —   —   —   —   —   —

Average Score
(AS) = TAS/N   —   —   —   —   —   —

Comments: _____

_____

Use asterisk to denote skill areas of instruction noted in the student's IEP for the year.
Refer to the CRS manual for calculation and interpretation.

LIFE CENTERED CAREER EDUCATION

Competency Rating Scale-Modified

Record Form

OCCUPATIONAL GUIDANCE AND PREPARATION

Student Name _____ Date of Birth _____ Sex _____

School _____City _____ State _____

Directions: Please rate the student according to his/her mastery of *each* item using the rating key below. Indicate the ratings in the column below the date for the rating period. Use the NR rating for items which cannot be rated. For subcompetencies rated 0 or 1 at the time of the final rating, place a check (✔) in the appropriate space in the *yes/no* column to indicate his/her ability to perform the subcompetency with assistance from the community. Please refer to the CRS manual for explanation of the rating key, description of the behavioral criteria for each subcompetency, and explanation of the *yes/no* column.

Rating Key: 0 = Not Competent   1 = Partially Competent   2 = Competent   NR = Not Related

To what extent has the student mastered the following subcompetencies?

Subcompetencies	Rater(s)									
	Grade Level									
	Date(s)									
OCCUPATIONAL GUIDANCE AND PREPARATION									*Yes*	*No*
15. *Exploring and Locating Occupational Training and Job Placement Opportunities*										
56. Identify Rewards of Working	___	___	___	___	___	___	___	___	___	
57. Locate Available Occupational Training and Job Placement Possibilities	___	___	___	___	___	___	___	___	___	
16. *Making Occupational Training and Job Placement Choices*										
58. Demonstrate Knowledge of Occupational Interests	___	___	___	___	___	___	___	___	___	
59. Demonstrate Knowledge of Occupational Strengths and Weaknesses	___	___	___	___	___	___	___	___	___	
60. Identify Possible and Available Jobs Matching Interests and Strengths	___	___	___	___	___	___	___	___	___	
61. Plan and Make Realistic Occupational Training and Job Placement Decisions	___	___	___	___	___	___	___	___	___	
62. Develop Training Plan for Occupational Choice	___	___	___	___	___	___	___	___	___	
17. *Applying for and Maintaining Occupational Training and Job Placement*										
63. Apply for Occupational Training and Job Placements	___	___	___	___	___	___	___	___	___	
64. Interview for Occupational Training and Job Placements	___	___	___	___	___	___	___	___	___	
65. Make Adjustments to Changes in Employment Status	___	___	___	___	___	___	___	___	___	

Subcompetencies	Rater(s)								
	Grade Level								
	Date(s)								
18. *Developing and Maintaining Appropriate Work Skills and Behavior*								Yes	No
66. Perform Work Directions and Meet Requirements	—	—	—	—	—	—	—	—	—
67. Maintain Good Attendance and Punctuality	—	—	—	—	—	—	—	—	—
68. Respond Approrpriately to Supervision	—	—	—	—	—	—	—	—	—
69. Demonstrate Job Safety	—	—	—	—	—	—	—	—	—
70. Work Cooperatively with Others	—	—	—	—	—	—	—	—	—
71. Meet Work Quality and Quantity Standards	—	—	—	—	—	—	—	—	—
19. *Matching Physical/Manual Skills to Occupational Training and Employment*									
72. Demonstrate Fine Motor Dexterity in Occupational Training and Job Placements	—	—	—	—	—	—	—	—	—
73. Demonstrate Gross Motor Dexterity in Occupational Training and Job Placements	—	—	—	—	—	—	—	—	—
74. Demonstrate Sensory Discrimination in Occupational Training and Job Placements	—	—	—	—	—	—	—	—	—
75. Demonstrate Stamina and Endurance	—	—	—	—	—	—	—	—	—
20. *Training for Occupational Skills* *There are no specific subcompetencies since they depend on the specific skill being taught.*									

Total Possible Score   Total Actual Score
   (TPS) = N 3 2 _____   (TAS)   —   —   —   —   —   —   —

                                    Average Score
                           (AS) = TAS/N   —   —   —   —   —   —   —

Cumulative TPS - 194   Cumulative TAS   —   —   —   —   —   —   —

                              Cumulative AS   —   —   —   —   —   —   —

Comments: _____

_____

Use asterisk to denote skill areas of instruction noted in the student's IEP for the year.
Refer to the CRS manual for calculation and interpretation.

Appendix C
Individualized Education
Program Form-Modified

The forms on the following pages are designed to be reproduced for use with the Life Centered Career Education (LCCE) Modified Curriculum.

LIFE CENTERED CAREER EDUCATION

Individualized Education Program Form-Modified
(Use attachments as needed for each student)

Student Name: _____ School: _____ Grade: _____ Date: _____

SECTION I: Present Level of Educational Performance

SECTION II: Annual Goals

A. Academic Goals (See attachment)

B. LCC Functional Skills for Transition Preparation (Check those that apply)
This student will progress toward acquiring functional behaviors in the following competency areas. (Check the appropriate annual goals.)

_____ 1. Managing Money
_____ 2. Selecting and Maintaining Living Environments
_____ 3. Caring for Personal Health
_____ 4. Developing and Maintaining Appropriate Intimate Relationships
_____ 5. Eating at Home and in the Community
_____ 6. Cleaning and Purchasing Clothing
_____ 7. Participate in Leisure/Recreational Activities
_____ 8. Traveling in the Community
_____ 9. Acquiring Self-Identity
_____ 10. Exhibiting Socially Responsible Behavior
_____ 11. Developing and Maintaining Appropriate Social Relationships
_____ 12. Exhibiting Independent Behavior

_____ 13. Making Informed Decisions
_____ 14. Communicating with Others
_____ 15. Exploring and Locating Occupational Training and Job Placement Opportunities
_____ 16. Making Occupational Training and Job Placement Choices
_____ 17. Applying for and Maintaining Occupational Training and Job Placements
_____ 18. Developing and Maintaining Appropriate Work Skills and Behavior
_____ 19. Matching Physical/Manual Skills to Occupational Training and Employment
_____ 20. Training for Occupational Choices

C. Other Transitional/Support Services Goals (Check those that apply)

_____ 1. Financial Assistance/Income Supprt
_____ 2. Advocacy Legal Services
_____ 3. Medical
_____ 4. Insurance

_____ 5. Transportation
_____ 6. Other _____
_____ 7. Other _____
_____ 8. Other _____

SECTION III: Specific Educational Services Needed

Goal & Subcomp. Numbers	Special Services Needed	Special Media/Materials and Equipment	Individual Implementors

Individualized Education Program Form-Modified

SECTION IV: Short-Term Individual Objectives

A. Academic Goals (see attachment)
B. LCCE Functional Skills for Transition Preparation (check those that apply)

_____ 1. Count Money
_____ 2. Make Purchase
_____ 3. Use Vending Machines
_____ 4. Budget Money
_____ 5. Perform Banking Skills
_____ 6. Select Appropriate Community Living Environments
_____ 7. Maintain Living Environments
_____ 8. Use Basic Appliances and Tools
_____ 9. Set Up Personal Living Space
_____ 10. Perform Appropriate Grooming and Hygiene
_____ 11. Dress Appropriately
_____ 12. Maintain Physical Fitness
_____ 13. Recognize and Seek Help for Illness
_____ 14. Practice Basic First Aid
_____ 15. Practice Personal Safety
_____ 16. Demonstrate Knowledge of Basic Human Sexuality
_____ 17. Demonstrate Knowledge of Appropriate Dating Behavior
_____ 18. Plan Balanced Meals
_____ 19. Purchase Food
_____ 20. Prepare Meals
_____ 21. Demonstrate Appropriate Eating Habits
_____ 22. Demonstrate Meal Clean-Up and Food Storage
_____ 23. Demonstrate Appropriate Restaurant Dining
_____ 24. Wash/Dry Clothes
_____ 25. Buy Clothes
_____ 26. Identify Available Community Leisure/Recreational Activities
_____ 27. Select and Plan Leisure/Recreational Activities
_____ 28. Participate in Individual and Group Leisure/Recreational Activities
_____ 29. Select and Participate in Group Travel
_____ 30. Follow Traffic Rules and Safety Procedures
_____ 31. Develop and Follow Community Access Routes
_____ 32. Access Available Transportation
_____ 33. Demonstrate Knowledge of Personal Interests and Abilities
_____ 34. Demonstrate Appropriate Responses to Emotions
_____ 35. Display Self-Confidence and Self-Worth
_____ 36. Demonstrate Giving and Accepting Praise and Criticism
_____ 37. Demonstrate Appropriate Behavior
_____ 38. Identify Current and Future Personal Roles
_____ 39. Demonstrate Respect for Other's Rights and Property
_____ 40. Demonstrate Respect for Authority
_____ 41. Demonstrate Ability to Follow Directions/Instructions

_____ 42. Demonstrate Appropriate Citizen Rights and Responsibilities
_____ 43. Identify How Personal Behavior Affects Others
_____ 44. Develop Friendships
_____ 45. Maintain Friendships
_____ 46. Set and Reach Personal Goals
_____ 47. Demonstrate Self-Organization
_____ 48. Demonstrate Self-Determination
_____ 49. Identify Problems/Conflicts
_____ 50. Use Appropriate Resources to Assist in Problem Solving
_____ 51. Develop and Select Best Solution to Problems/Conflicts
_____ 52. Demonstrate Decision Making
_____ 53. Demonstrate Listening and Responding Skills
_____ 54. Demonstrate Effective Communication
_____ 55. Communicate in Emergency Situations
_____ 56. Identify Rewards of Working
_____ 57. Locate Available Occupational Training and Job Placement Possibilities
_____ 58. Demonstrate Knowledge of Occupational Interests
_____ 59. Demonstrate Knowledge of Occupational Strengths and Weaknesses
_____ 60. Identify Possible and Available Jobs Matching Interests and Strengths
_____ 61. Plan and Make Realistic Occupational Training and Job Placement Decisions
_____ 62. Develop Training Plan for Occupational Choice
_____ 63. Apply for Occupational Training and Job Placements
_____ 64. Interview for Occupational Training and Job Placements
_____ 65. Make Adjustments to Changes in Employment Status
_____ 66. Perform Work Directions and Meet Requirements
_____ 67. Maintain Good Attendance and Punctuality
_____ 68. Respond Approrpriately to Supervision
_____ 69. Demonstrate Job Safety
_____ 70. Work Cooperatively with Others
_____ 71. Meet Work Quality and Quantity Standards
_____ 72. Demonstrate Fine Motor Dexterity in Occupational Training and Job Placements
_____ 73. Demonstrate Gross Motor Dexterity in Occupational Training and Job Placements
_____ 74. Demonstrate Sensory Discrimination in Occupational Training and Job Placements
_____ 75. Demonstrate Stamina and Endurance

Individualized Education Program Form-Modified

SECTION V: Date and Length of Time relative to specific educational services needed for this student

Goal Number	Beginning Date	Ending Date		Goal Number	Beginning Date	Ending Date

SECTION VI: Description of Extent to which this student will participate in the regular educational program

	Percentage of Time	*Narrative Description/Reaction*
Language arts	_____%	
Math	_____%	
Science	_____%	
Social science	_____%	
Vocational (Bus.) & Work Study	_____%	
Physical education	_____%	
(other) _____	_____%	
(other) _____	_____%	

SECTION VII: Justification for type of educational placement of this student

Narrative Description/Reaction

Individualized Education Program Form-Modified

SECTION VIII: Individual Responsible for implementing the individualized education program and transitional services

        Name   *Role/Responsibility*

SECTION IX: Objective Criteria, Evaluation Procedures, and Schedule for assessing short-term objectives

Objective criteria can be found in the LCCE Competency Rating Scale (CRS), the LCCE Knowledge Battery (KB), and the LCCE Performance Battery (PB). Criteria listed reflect the short-term individual objectives checked in Section IV, Part B, of this form.

Evaulation Procedures can be determined by the IEP Committee reviewing the manuals for the Competency Rating Scale, Knowledge Battery, and Performance Battery.

Schedule for Assessment should include time, date, frequency, place, etc.

SECTION X: Estimated Date, Location, and Time for next IEP Committee Review

Appendix D
LCCE Resources
Available from CEC

Life Centered Career Education: A Competency Based Approach
Fifth Edition
Donn E. Brolin

The fifth edition of the basic LCCE text includes improvements that make it easier to use in conjunction with the LCCE Complete Curriculum Package. Pages have been tabbed for quick reference to the Daily Living, Personal-Social, and Occupational Guidance and Preparation domains. Objectives have been numbered to coincide with the lesson plans in the Complete Curriculum Package. The competencies have remained the same, and the 97 subcompetencies and over 400 objectives continue to provide the most comprehensive career education program available. The guide also contains the Competency Rating Scale (CRS), a subjective assessment instrument used to rate student achievement. This is a very useful screening device and is extremely helpful in selecting areas for instructional planning.

No. P180G. 1997. 175 pp. ISBN 0-86586-292-3. $30, CEC Members $21

Life Centered Career Education
Modified Curriculum for Individuals with Moderate Disabilities
Robert J. Loyd and Donn E. Brolin

This modified version of the LCCE Curriculum provides practitioners with the same easy-to-use format of the original text. A correlation table allows teachers to identify corresponding competencies in each curriculum in the event that students are able to move from this more basic version to the more advanced objectives of the original work. The major difference between the original and the modified curriculum programs is that the modified curriculum focuses on the critical skills and outcomes that individuals with moderate disabilities need to perform to assist them in making a successful transition from school to work and community living. Another significant difference is that attention to both support needed and participation levels is embedded in the curriculum activities and individuals are encouraged to seek assistance when necessary. A modified Competency Rating Scale (CRS) is included in the text. This instrument is useful in determining appropriate objectives to be included in the IEP or other planning documents.

No. P5194. 1997. 107 pp. ISBN 0-86586-293-1. $30, CEC Members $21

LCCE Demonstration Video
This 55-minute video provides an explanation of the LCCE curriculum and demonstrates administration of the Knowledge and Performance Batteries as well as a number of instructional lessons. This product can be used to support inservice training or to model teaching and testing strategies to teachers who are new to the program. The video follows the content of LCCE Training Workshops.

No. M5189. Edited 1996. 55 min. VHS. $75

The IEP Planner for LCCE Transition Skills
Allows teachers to incorporate Life Centered Career Education (LCCE) skills into students' IEPs. Each competency from the LCCE Curriculum is listed along with up to 9 objectives for each of the 97 competencies—more than 400 objectives altogether. The program allows teachers to edit any objective or add special goals and objectives as needed. Easy to update for annual reviews and progress reports. You can even import your own district's curriculum. The package includes:

* Disks for both Macintosh and DOS-based computers containing LCCE objectives and an IEP form template.
* A spiral bound book of codes for LCCE competencies and goals and the IEP form.
* A copy of Life Centered Career Education: A Competency Based Approach, the foundation text by Donn E. Brolin.

No. S5174. 1996. $220

Life Centered Career Education
The Complete Curriculum and Assessment Package
Includes over 1,100 lesson plans covering Daily Living Skills, Personal-Social Skills, and Occupational Skills; Knowledge Batteries (10 copies of each of two alternative forms); Performance Batteries; Administration Manuals; and Technical Report.

No. P371. 1992. $980

LCCE: Daily Living Skills
Donn E. Brolin

Includes 472 lesson plans covering personal finances, household management, personal needs, family responsibilities, food preparation, citizenship responsibilities, and leisure.

No. P367. 1992. 1,556 pp. 3 loose-leaf binders. ISBN 0-86586-224-9. $400

LCCE: Personal-Social Skills
Donn E. Brolin

Provides 370 lesson plans for developing self-awareness, self-confidence, socially responsible behavior, good interpersonal skills, independence, decision-making, and communication skills.

No. P368. 1992. 1,348 pp. 3 loose-leaf binders. ISBN 0-86586-225-7. $400

LCCE: Occupational Guidance and Preparation
Richard T. Roessler and Donn E. Brolin

Includes 286 lesson plans to help students explore occupational possibilities; make occupational choices; develop appropriate work habits; seek, secure, and maintain employment; exhibit sufficient physical/manual skills; and obtain specific occupational competencies.

No. P369. 1992. 670 pp. 2 loose-leaf binders. ISBN 0-86586-226-5. $300

LCCE: Competency Assessment Knowledge Batteries
Available in parallel forms, each Knowledge Battery consists of 200 multiple-choice questions that cover the first 20 competencies. Primarily a screening instrument, the Knowledge Batteries were designed to pinpoint specific competency deficiencies. Package includes an Administration Manual, a Technical Report, and samples of each form of the test. Also included are two introductory sets of 10 Knowledge Batteries, Forms A and B, to use with students.

No. P370K. 1992. 152 pp. ISBN 0-86586-239-7. $125

LCCE: Competency Assessment Performance Batteries
The Performance Batteries consist of two alternative forms for each of the 21 competency units. Items are primarily performance based and should be administered to students before and after instructional units have been taught. Performance Batteries are administered individually or with small groups of students. Test materials must be reproduced as needed. Performance Batteries are packaged in a loose-leaf binder along with an Administration Manual.

No. P370P. 1992. 675 pp. ISBN 0-86586-240-0. $225

Additional Sets of Knowledge Batteries
Packages of 10 tests may be ordered separately to be used by students. Students may answer questions directly in the test booklets by circling the correct choice or may use a standard machine-scorable form. Knowledge Batteries may not be reproduced.

LCCE: Knowledge Battery Form A (10 per package) No. P372. $20

LCCE: Knowledge Battery Form B (10 per package) No. P373. $20

Prices change without notice. Please call 1-800-CEC-READ (232-7323) to confirm prices and shipping charges.

LCCE On-site training is also available. For more information about LCCE workshops, regional events, and technical assistance, call 703-264-9451.

Council for Exceptional Children
1110 North Glebe Road, Suite 300
Arlington, VA 22201-5704
1-800-232-7323
Fax: 703-264-9494